THE BEST JOURNEY EVER:
A SIMPLE GUIDE THROUGH CHRISTIANITY

P. L. BENNETT

First published 2021
by Rowanvale Books Ltd
The Gate
Keppoch Street
Roath
Cardiff
CF24 3JW
www.rowanvalebooks.com

A CIP catalogue record for this book is available from the British Library.

ISBN: 978-1-913662-11-0

DEDICATION

The Best Journey Ever: A Simple Guide Through Christianity, was written through inspiration and guidance of the Holy Spirit. All the praise goes to God for His purpose in my life. I am blessed to be surrounded by some special people who God has placed in my life and who continue to encourage me in my endeavours.

My special love and thanks to my daughter, Paige Lewin, who is so full of encouragement, support and determination and Tom Proudley. Both convinced me never to give up on this journey. I am indebted to Shelley Sohal, Whitney O'Connor, Lisha Batchelor, Vivinne Bramwell, Malvia Henry and Maxine McKen. Thank you for allowing me to glean so much from your enquiring minds and answering questions that formed the foundation for this book.

I would like to thank my sister, Marie Bennett, for her support and encouragement in helping me to identify the need for a simple guide to help others understand the Christian faith.

I thank you all for the hours of your time taken in reading these chapters and working to my very demanding deadlines, providing me with priceless feedback and constructive advice and your unwavering belief that this guide is needed.

Thank you all for your love and support!

CONTENTS

INTRODUCTION

When a baby is born, you wouldn't send them out into the world to live their life, feed and teach themselves, and expect them to know how to deal with the unexpected. In much the same way, when someone makes the decision to become a Christian and start their journey as a babe in Christ, we should not expect the same of them. Someone at the beginning of their Christian journey is not yet fully equipped for the journey, so they need help, which comes from the preachers, teachers and nurturers whom God has called upon to support that person to maturity.

During their first few years after becoming a Christian, some people become rooted very quickly and go from strength to strength, while some fall away and others barely 'hang in there'. Whichever category they fall into, every person beginning their Christian journey needs help and support. Jesus knew this when He directed Peter to feed His lambs and feed His sheep, referring to the new and not-so-new Christians. This support needs to start from the moment a person makes that commitment and should continue throughout their Christian life.

It is vital to understand your faith and become rooted in it from the outset. Once a decision has been made to follow Christ and the new convert begins that journey, it is not an easy one and it doesn't help that we complicate it by creating our own rules in order to fulfil our own desires and our own will instead of God's. For those who struggle or fall away there seems to be very little that anyone is able to do to help them. Having mentored and counselled many new Christians who were struggling on their journey of faith, I decided to dig a little deeper to try to understand the real dynamics of what was happening. The reasons were the same again and again. Some felt that, in the first two to three years after being baptised, they had not grown spiritually but had remained stagnant or actually gone backwards. Many struggled with Christian concepts, did not know how to pray, did not understand the Bible or how to study it and, on the occasions when they did open the pages, were even more bewildered after closing them.

The concept of fasting was a mystery to many, while by far the most challenging of all the struggles was that many Christians did not know what their purpose was or why they were called into the kingdom. The 'Why am I here?' was still a problem in their lives. Many had not received the baptism of the Holy Spirit with the evidence of speaking in tongues and were as baffled by the Holy Spirit as the world was. The answers were the same whoever I asked and wherever they worshipped—their struggles were real!

Being led by the Holy Spirit to approach some of our church's new members who came and went every Sunday, speaking to no one and having no one speak to them, I was saddened that they did not seem to be a part of the church community. After the initial excitement of the water baptism, and the welcoming embraces, many new Christians felt lonely, alienated, overwhelmed with the pace of their new life and unable to initiate conversations with others that they did not know well. They were suddenly being told to pray, fast, read their Bible, live right, don't do this, don't do that and turn up to church every Sunday, but with little personalised help and guidance on how to really start living this life.

To balance the argument, churches do have weekly worship, Bible studies, various study groups, and many group activities that the new convert can be a part of. So why were they still feeling alienated and falling away? During my discussions with many new Christians, I found that, whilst there is no single reason for this, the primary struggle that caused a blockage in their spiritual growth was a real lack of understanding of the Christian faith and the role they were expected to play in it. This was followed closely by the pace of life and expectations; too fast and too great.

Those converts who had been on the journey for a while or understood their purpose kept going, while the new ones were expected to join in and 'keep up'. The new converts were not being treated like babes in Christ at all but more like mature Christians. Group sessions were pre-planned, not leaving room for questions on other topics or concerns; asking questions in a large group was daunting and there was little or no platform for personal questions. Our efforts as mature Christians are definitely not enough— something is clearly missing.

Amid this world of confusion, Christians are struggling or falling away from the faith, others don't know what to believe in, while many are being deceived and suffering needlessly. A greater understanding is needed to help many find their way to God, or back to Him. However, if someone doesn't want to know or doesn't fully understand this journey, no one can force it on them. We can only help someone who wants to be helped. *The Best Journey Ever* provides a simple guide through the Christian Journey—if you are willing to take it.

CHAPTER 1
HOW IT ALL STARTED

"I am Alpha and Omega, the beginning and the end,
the first and the last."

Revelation 22:13 KJV

The Godhead

Two of the most profound questions I have been asked by someone who was not a Christian but wanted to know more were simply, "Where did it all begin? What's it all about?"

So few people ask these questions, although they are definitely the only starting point in understanding Christianity. Without the full picture, or at least an overview of it, there will always be gaps in a new Christian's understanding. Here we start at the beginning.

Before a new Christian or a non-Christian can begin to understand the need to be 'saved' and the ultimate reward of eternal life in the presence of God, they need to understand the foundations on which the faith is built and why there is a need for it in the first place.

The source of all things—power, life force, the world as we know it—is God. There is one God, in three distinct persons. God the Father, God the Son and God the Holy Spirit, referred to as 'The Holy Trinity' or the 'Triune God'.

These three Persons make up the Godhead. What a lot of people don't realise is that God is a title, not a name, and in that title is His divine nature, that of a supreme being. The greatest revelation of the nature of God is seen through His Son, Jesus. So how is it possible to have one God in three persons? The simple answer is that the three persons of the Godhead are 'ONE' in 'purpose' and 'will'. In

John 10:30, Jesus declares to the people when they continue to challenge Him, "I and My Father are one." He explains this so beautifully in the following scripture:

"Jesus said to him, 'Have I been with you for so long a time, and you do not know Me yet, Philip, nor recognise clearly who I am? Anyone who has seen Me has seen the Father. How can you say, "Show us the Father?" Do you not believe that I am in the Father, and the Father is in Me? The words I say to you I do not say on My own initiative or authority, but the Father, abiding continually in Me, does His works [His attesting miracles and acts of power].'"

[John 14:9-10 AMP]

So, Jesus and God the Father are one because They are in perfect agreement with each other. Jesus does the work of the Father and the only way we can get to the Father is through Him. "Jesus said to him [Thomas], 'I am the way, the truth, and the life: no man comes to the Father but by Me.'"

[John 14:6 NKJV]

The only way to the Father is through the Son and this can only happen when the Holy Spirit draws us to Him. All three persons work together for one purpose: to save souls and bring them into the kingdom of heaven and into the presence of God the Father. The baptism of Jesus, which is described to us in the four gospels of the New Testament (Matthew, Mark, Luke and John), reveals the Holy Trinity working in perfect unity:

"After Jesus was baptised, He came up immediately out of the water; and behold, the heavens were opened, and he [John] saw the Spirit of God descending as a dove and lighting on Him [Jesus], and behold, a voice from heaven said, 'This is My beloved Son, in whom I am well-pleased and delighted!'"

[Matthew 3:16-17 AMP]

God is self-existing and has existed in three persons since before our time began. The following scripture tells us that God is the beginning, the end, the first and the last:

"I am the Alpha and the Omega, the First and the Last, the Beginning and the End [the Eternal One]."

[Revelation 22:13 AMP]

The Godhead always works as one in perfect unity; there is never a deviation from God the Father's plan. When many people say God, they think only of God the Father, but we must remember that Jesus and the Holy Spirit are God also. They exist not as three gods but as one God in three persons; one title innate in all three persons. If you refer to God the Father as God, God the Son as Jesus and God the Holy Spirit as the Holy Spirit, that is absolutely fine and easily clarifies whom you are speaking to and about; but know that they are all God, whether we choose to acknowledge this or not.

An example of two persons being classed as one is when two people get married. They still remain as two distinct persons with their separate personalities, but now they are one in purpose, which is to love and cherish each other, to respect each other and to work towards a unified goal for the rest of their lives. Although this doesn't happen as often as it should today, this is how God intended it to be. Jesus explains this to the religious leaders of the time who were constantly challenging Him:

"He replied, 'Have you never read that He who created them from the beginning made them male and female, and said, "For this reason a man shall leave his father and mother and shall be joined inseparably to his wife, and the two shall become one flesh?" So they are no longer two, but one flesh. Therefore, what God has joined together, let no one separate.'"

[Matthew 19:4-6 AMP]

So Jesus confirms that God made a male and a female in the beginning, so that they can come together and be unified in marriage, becoming one flesh. The oneness is both a spiritual and a physical bonding, representing the fact that they should be intimate with only each other and not any third parties. So the Godhead works in unity at all times for a single purpose—one will, one goal—which will become apparent as you continue to read.

God the Father
God the Father is the source of all things. He has many names, such as Jehovah, Adonai and I AM, but the one I have found most people to be familiar with is Jehovah.

"That men may know that You, whose name alone is Jehovah, are the Most High over all the Earth."

[Psalms 83:18 KJV]

The universe, everything we are and everything we know—the planets, the sun and the moon, the blue skies, the expansive seas, the elevated mountains, the wind, the rain, the animals, the air that we breathe, mankind as we know it—all were created by God, Jehovah, the one true, living God.

FACT

A very important point to make here is not to confuse God, Jehovah, with any gods from other religions or faiths. Often people will try to convince you that Jehovah and Allah are one and the same and that they are just different names for the same God; this is not true!

It is important to study the Holy Bible to prevent yourself from being deceived by popular beliefs. Just because a belief is popular doesn't make it true; it is simply easier to go with the grain than to go against it as there are fewer challenges and less controversy. The Christian life, however, is not about going with the grain or aligning with popular beliefs. Jesus did not align Himself with the popular beliefs and cultures of His time and many refused to accept the doctrines He taught. When you begin to read the Bible, the Holy Spirit will reveal truths to you, so you will be able to identify the ways that are not of the Lord. Don't follow the crowd, follow the truth!

We cannot see God, but we know He is here and there, He is omnipresent, which is to be in all places at the same time. He is omnipotent, which is supreme and all-powerful, and He is omniscient—he knows all things. We often wonder what God the Father looks like, because no physical being has ever seen Him. The Bible tells us that God is a spirit and, although He is invisible to us, we know He has a form; He has a spiritual body. When Moses asked God if he could see Him, the Lord responded:

"'You cannot see My face, for no man shall see Me and live!' Then the Lord said, 'Behold, there is a place beside Me, and you shall stand there on the rock; and while My glory is passing by, I will put you in a cleft of the rock and protectively cover you with My hand until I have passed by. Then I will take away My hand and you shall see My back; but My face shall not be seen."

[Exodus 33:20-23 AMP]

Here, we have confirmation from God Himself that He has a face, hands, front and back parts. He confirms that, if a human being looks at Him, they cannot survive it because His power and His glory are too much for the physical body and mind to comprehend. In the book of Genesis (meaning *the origin, creation*—the first book of the Bible), God tells us:

"Let Us make man in Our image, according to Our likeness."

[Genesis 1:26 NKJV]

So, we know that our physical form was created in the image of God. This passage also confirms that God the Father was not referring to just Himself when deciding to create us. He said, 'let Us' and 'Our image', so again we see the Godhead working in perfect unity in the creation of mankind. We look like our Creator, but let us not confuse ourselves by saying our Creator looks like us. The child looks like the parent and not the other way around; we respect and revere our Father in heaven. We also know that God has a heart, senses and feelings and awesome power, as told to us in the following scripture after Noah offered burnt offerings on an altar he'd built for God:

"And the Lord smelled a soothing aroma. Then the Lord said in His heart, 'I will never again curse the ground for man's sake, although the imagination of man's heart is evil from his youth; nor will I again destroy every living thing as I have done.'"

[Genesis 8:21 NKJV]

Every generation appears to have grown more distant from God and seems to love God less, even though He continues to love us all with a passion. The world has come to a point where there is a greater belief in the characters and messages of fictional books than the Bible and its teachings. Yet through all this God remains unchangeable. We read that God is love, but how often do we take a moment to think about what this really means? God loves us and this has not changed through time. But He doesn't just love us, for He Himself is love. The following scripture confirms this:

"Beloved, let us love one another, for love is of God; and everyone who loves is born of God and knows God. He who does not love does not know God, for God is love."

[1 John 4:7-8 NKJV]

A good way to begin to understand this is to reflect on the character and nature of God, the things He has done and the things He continues to do for us. We have a Father who created us, the universe and all things in it. A Father who allowed us to kill His only Son to save us, the very people who killed Him, so that we could have a relationship with Him once more. With all the power that God has, He only does good, shows mercy and forgives us when He doesn't have to. He owes us nothing, yet He continues to work patiently with us.

Ask yourselves which king, queen, president, prime minister or 'powerful ruler' on this Earth has ever come close to loving their subjects or followers in the way that God loves us? Which leader with status, riches, power and influence would allow themselves to be humiliated by the people they are ruling over? None!

Great leaders have consistently misused their power in one way or another, publicly or behind closed doors. Yet God, with all of His power, chooses not to make our lives a misery but instead to give us a second chance. He chooses to forgive us continually and is not corrupted by that power. Everything God does is from a place of love, so love is His very nature. His thoughts towards us are always of love, so He doesn't just love us, He *is* that love; and it is that love that forms the foundation on which Christianity is built.

God the Son

God the Son is called Jesus. He is the divine Son of Jehovah. His name means 'Jehovah is salvation', and salvation means to be rescued, delivered or saved. It is for this reason that Jesus had to be born into mankind, to save us from ourselves. The angel of the Lord spoke to Joseph about Mary's pregnancy, telling him:

"She will give birth to a Son, and you shall name Him Jesus [The Lord is salvation], for He will save His people from their sins."

[Matthew 1:21 AMP]

Joseph and Mary were Jesus' earthly parents. Many people think that Christ is Jesus' last name, but this is incorrect. Jesus does not have a last name and in His own time was simply called Jesus of Nazareth. Christ is a title and it means 'Anointed One' (or, in Hebrew, Messiah). When we say Jesus Christ, we are saying Jesus, the Anointed One. In that title is the nature of Jesus as He is not just an Anointed One, but He is The Anointed One of God—there is no other. This means that God the Father set Jesus apart for a specific purpose, and that was to save the world and to provide an escape route for us out of sin (lawlessness, wrongdoings and immorality). To sin is to miss the mark which is God's standard.

Jesus, like His Father, has many names, but one that many people find confusing is when He is referred to as the 'Word of God'. God's Word is the Holy Bible. It is life to the Christian, it is the perfect will of God, it is food to our spirit, it empowers us, it heals, it prophesies the future and the first and second coming of Christ. Jesus is the Word of God in the flesh. He represents God's perfection in all His ways. When Jesus came to us, He fulfilled everything that was foretold in the scriptures.

The Book of John (the fourth book of the New Testament) confirms Jesus as the Word of God and affirms that He was not created as humans were, but existed from the beginning with God. "In the beginning [before all time] was the Word [Christ], and the Word was with God, and the Word was God Himself. He was [continually existing] in the beginning [co-eternally] with God."

[John 1:1-2 AMP]

"And the Word [Christ] became flesh, and lived among us; and we [actually] saw His glory, glory as belongs to the [One and] only begotten Son of the Father, [the Son who is truly unique, the only One of His kind, who is] full of grace and truth [absolutely free of deception]."

[John 1:14 AMP]

Many believe that Jesus came into existence when He was born on the Earth some two thousand years ago, but this was when He took on a physical form and became a man, not the start of His existence. Jesus was sent down to Earth by God to undo the damage that was done to mankind by Satan, the devil, and to help us out of the sinful state that we put ourselves in. He is the Son of the Living God, so don't be afraid to declare it.

God the Holy Spirit

God the Holy Spirit is called the Holy Spirit or the Spirit of Truth and is the Spirit of God. We know that, in the beginning, when God created the world, the Holy Spirit was present and active.

"The Spirit of God was moving [hovering, brooding] over the face of the waters."

[Genesis 1:2 AMP]

God the Father was never alone; Jesus and the Holy Spirit have been with Him since before the beginning of (our) time. Many people will say that they know of God and they know of Jesus, but when the Holy Spirit is mentioned, that's where we lose them. Many Christians, regardless of their denominations, are baffled by Him. They can accept that God and Jesus are in heaven, but the Holy Spirit of God who dwells within us on the Earth is a genuine challenge for many. Jesus speaks of the Holy Spirit many times and comforts His disciples as His imminent departure approaches:

"And I will ask the Father, and He will give you another Helper [Comforter, Advocate, Intercessor, Counsellor, Strengthener, Standby], to be with you forever..."

[John 14:16 AMP]

Christ also says that the world cannot accept the Holy Spirit because they don't know Him. If they haven't accepted Christ, they cannot accept the Holy Spirit. Indeed, some who do accept Christ still cannot accept the Holy Spirit.

"The Spirit of Truth, whom the world cannot receive [and take to its heart] because it does not see Him or know Him; but you know Him because He [the Holy Spirit] remains with you continually and will be in you."

[John 14:17 AMP]

He dwells within us, but not against our will, only when we accept Jesus as our Lord and Saviour and ask Him to fill us with His holy presence. Although the world may not know the Holy Spirit, we as Christians should. If you are a Christian and have no idea who the Holy Spirit is, ask Him to reveal Himself to you. Remember He is God the Holy Spirit. Proving that the Holy Spirit exists is like trying to prove God the Father exists; it's an impossible task which has not been given to us. Instead, focus on experiencing the Holy Spirit for yourself and don't worry about trying to convince others that He exists!

FACT

One very important fact to remember here is that the Holy Spirit is a living being, the divine Holy Spirit of God, and should never be referred to as 'it'. 'It' is an inanimate object without thoughts, feelings or will, not a person. The Holy Spirit of God is a He!

The Holy Spirit empowers us for the spiritual journey ahead. When we pray to God in the name of Jesus, the power and authority comes from God the Father through the Son, who instructs the Holy Spirit to carry out the work in us. Jesus, before He was taken up into heaven, told the disciples:
"But you will receive power and ability when the Holy Spirit comes upon you."

[Acts 1:8 AMP]

Without the Holy Spirit, our Christian lives are average. With the Holy Spirit we can reach for the stars—the possibilities are endless. Only through Him can we find our purpose and fulfil our destiny.

Our Beginnings

In the beginning, God created a perfect world. He created the heavens, the moon, the stars, the sun, the seas and everything in them. He created the trees and plants in the earth, the animals and mankind, starting with Adam and Eve. In that world, He created a garden in Eden and put Adam in it to live and to tend it. But God decided that it was not good for Adam to be on his own, so He created a woman, whom Adam named Eve, to be his wife.

God loved His creation and saw that it was good—perfect people who did not kill animals, not even for food, and animals who did not kill the humans who had power over them. Killing was not necessary because all created life had everything they could ever need; the world was in perfect equilibrium. There was no death, no sickness, no sin in any shape or form. Sin goes against the divine law of God. The world was created by God, who simply spoke things into being, so something that did not exist or could not be seen came into existence through the power and authority of God's spoken Word. Throughout Genesis 1 and 2, God said "Let there be..." each time He created something, and it came into being.

FACT

Creation is the beginning of this world as we know it and the origin of humans. This was not the beginning of all time, because God existed before this time.

Man, however, was not created from the spoken Word; we were formed from something that already existed – the earth. Adam, his name meaning red ground, was made from the raw material of the ground:
"Then the Lord God formed [that is, created the body of] man from the dust of the ground, and breathed into his nostrils the breath of life; and the man became a living being [an individual complete in body and spirit]."

[Genesis 2:7 AMP]

When the Lord God breathed His life force into Adam, Adam became a living, breathing, fully-grown adult. In potentially fatal situations when someone stops breathing, the ultimate act we perform is to breathe our breath of life into them by giving them mouth-to-mouth resuscitation. It comes naturally to us because that is how we came into being.

God also breathed His genetic makeup into us—we have our Father's DNA. We don't just look like God, we also have the capacity to be like Him in the things that we say and do. We did not evolve over a period as evolution teaches, so the answer to the question, "which came first, the chicken or the egg?" is undeniably the chicken. All life was created as fully-grown adults and blessed with the ability to reproduce.

So, God created us as His children and loves us with a passion. All He asks is for us to love Him, just as you would expect in any parent-child relationship. Adam and Eve were created naked, just as new babies are born naked. Totally innocent, they were clothed in God's Glory and had everything they could ever need. The herbs, fruits and produce from the trees provided both the humans and animals with plenty of food. At that time, animals were not killed for meat. The garden planted in Eden was home for Adam and his family.

The book of Genesis (the first book of the Bible) describes the beauty of the Earth and what life was like during the time of Adam and Eve. God indulged Adam and let him name all the animals and creatures that He (God) had created. Adam also named Eve, meaning *life spring* or *life giver*, because she was the mother of all life [Genesis 3:20 AMP], and called her 'woman', because she was taken out of the man. Life in God's garden was awesome, amazing and peaceful. A distant world from the one we live in today.

The Bible does not tell us how long Adam and Eve lived in the garden before everything went wrong, but it does tell us what went wrong.

Who is Satan?

The original sin was born in Satan, which means 'adversary'. He is the enemy and constant challenger of God. Satan is the personal name of the devil, often referred to as 'the enemy', a term many people seem better able to cope with. The devil is often believed to be a fantasy figure, a fairy tale that's not real, but alas, the devil is real. He exists. You cannot in all honesty believe in God and not believe that there is a devil. Please don't worship him, just know that he is real and very harmful. Whilst we do not fear him as Christians, we do not dismiss the fact that he is alive and causing a great deal of damage. Satan was an archangel, so he was the head of multitudes of angels. The following scripture describes who Satan was before he became evil and was thrown out of heaven:

"You had the full measure of perfection and the finishing touch [of completeness],

Full of wisdom and perfect in beauty.

You were in Eden, the garden of God [not the Garden of Eden where Adam and Eve lived];

Every precious stone was your covering:

The ruby, the topaz, and the diamond;
The beryl, the onyx, and the jasper;
The lapis lazuli, the turquoise, and the emerald;
And the gold, the workmanship of your settings and your sockets,
Was in you.
They were prepared
On the day that you were created.
You were the anointed cherub [angel] who covers and protects [covering angel, archangel],
And I placed you there.
You were on the holy mountain of God; You walked in the midst of the stones of fire [sparkling jewels].
You were blameless in your ways
From the day you were created
Until unrighteousness and evil were found in you."

[Ezekiel 28:12-15 AMP]

Satan was beautiful and placed in a position of authority over other angels. His name was Lucifer, meaning 'bearer of light' or 'morning star' and, before he sinned, he lived in the heavens with God, praising and worshipping God.

Lucifer, however, started to believe that he could compete with God and, as a result of his beliefs, his heart became filled with sinful desires against God. God deals with the heart, so He knew what Lucifer was thinking even before Lucifer was able to act on it.
"But you said in your heart,
'I will ascend to heaven;
I will raise my throne above the stars of God;
I will sit on the mount of assembly
In the remote parts of the north.
I will ascend above the heights of the clouds;
I will make myself like the Most High.'
But [in fact] you will be brought down to Sheol,
To the remote recesses of the pit [the region of the dead]."

[Isaiah 14:13-15 AMP]

We know from the scripture above that Lucifer was prideful and vain in planning to overthrow God. Pride is a feeling of deep pleasure or satisfaction in your own achievements. It is thinking that you possess qualities and beauty greatly admired and desired by others, and basking in it. Vanity is excessive pride in or admiration of your own achievements; it is self-indulgent and goes hand in hand with pride. Such were Lucifer's pride and vanity that he sought to use God's angels against Him. It was so destructive that he believed that he, a created being, could overpower God, who had created him. The deep desire in Lucifer's heart was to be 'like' the Most High—God.

The problem with pride, if we allow it to be rooted in our hearts, is that all logic and reason goes out the window as we are driven by our desires, which makes it very difficult to identify this flaw in ourselves. The saying "pride comes before a fall" is perfectly demonstrated here by Lucifer before he was thrown out of heaven. He said "I will" five times in his heart. He made everything about him, and the consequence of this was that he caused a great battle to be fought in the heavens and was responsible for the falling away of one third of the angels of heaven, who followed him to everlasting ruin:

"... a great fiery red dragon [Satan] with seven heads and ten horns, and on his heads were seven royal crowns [diadems]. And his tail swept [across the sky] and dragged away a third of the stars of heaven and flung them to the earth."

[Revelation 12:3-4 AMP]

Everyone to some extent has a level of pride. We may take pride in the way we look or in our children, our home, our achievements and possessions. This is natural until it becomes excessive and harmful to us and to others. A prideful person seeking power will always drag others down with them because they cannot achieve it by themselves. Power and control over nations requires an army, so Lucifer must have been very convincing for a third of the angels to follow him to certain doom in revolting against God.

God himself did not fight Lucifer. Instead, it was Michael, one of the archangels, head of the army of warrior angels, who defeated Lucifer and his followers.

"And war broke out in heaven, Michael [the archangel] and his angels waging war with the dragon. The dragon and his angels fought, but they were not strong enough and did not prevail, and there was no longer a place found for them in heaven. And the great dragon was thrown down, the age-old serpent who is called the devil and Satan, he who continually deceives and seduces the entire inhabited world; he was thrown down to the earth, and his angels were thrown down with him."

[Revelation 12:7-9 AMP]

Satan lost the battle that day so decided to challenge God constantly. He cannot harm or kill God, so he tries to destroy God's most precious creation—mankind. And all because he thought (and continues to think) he is more than he is—this is pride. Satan cares for nothing and no one and, even though he knows his end will be bitter, he doesn't care. His aim is to take down as many souls with him as possible. He cannot be reasoned with! So, the beauty of Lucifer diminishes, replaced by ugliness. He is now referred to as the dragon, that serpent, the devil and Satan.

There is no indication in the Bible that Lucifer asked for forgiveness or that he would receive it if he did. God cannot lie and the Bible is His perfect Word, and it tells us that Lucifer will burn for all eternity in the lake of fire, so we know there is no forgiveness for him. The reason there is no forgiveness for Satan and why he is so repulsive to God is because he always challenges Him. He tries to destroy everything that God creates, ultimately attempting to put himself on God's level. It is on this premise that man fell, and Christianity came into being.

The Fall of Mankind

As stated before, when God created Adam He put him in the garden to tend and keep it. God would go to the garden regularly to spend time with Adam, talking to him as a father would to a son. God loved and indulged Adam by letting him name all the animals that were created. God then created a wife for Adam, blessed them and told them to "be fruitful and multiply". They were free to love, have children, travel and discover the beauty of the Earth. There was, however, one condition placed on Adam and Eve in order to protect them. Just one:

"And the Lord God commanded the man, saying, 'You may freely [unconditionally] eat [the fruit] from every tree of the garden; but

[only] from the tree of the knowledge [recognition] of good and evil you shall not eat, otherwise on the day that you eat from it, you shall most certainly die [because of your disobedience]."'

[Genesis 2:16-17 AMP]

FACT

Now just to be clear, the tree of "Life" was also in the middle of the garden next to the tree of the knowledge of good and evil, and Adam and Eve were free to eat the fruits from that tree. This would have given mankind eternal life in their perfection. But that tree was ignored!

Satan, having been flung unceremoniously out of heaven, has only hatred in his heart for us because we were created so perfectly in God's own image and likeness and are so loved by Him. To be created in the image of God was too great an honour for Satan to ignore. The hatred he has for God and God's creation was too much for him. He plotted against us, using the serpent to befriend and entice Eve to be disobedient to God, who then encouraged her husband to do the same, ultimately taking our birthright from us. The following scripture tells us how he did it: "Now the serpent was more crafty [subtle, skilled in deceit] than any living creature of the field which the Lord God had made. And the serpent [Satan] said to the woman, 'Can it really be that God has said, "You shall not eat from any tree of the garden"?' And the woman said to the serpent, 'We may eat fruit from the trees of the garden, except the fruit from the tree which is in the middle of the garden. God said, "You shall not eat from it nor touch it, otherwise you will die."' But the serpent said to the woman, 'You certainly will not die! For God knows that on the day you eat from it your eyes will be opened [that is, you will have greater awareness], and you will be like God, knowing [the difference between] good and evil.'"

[Genesis 3:1-5 AMP]

It is impossible to grasp the sadness in God's heart as the events unfolded, but because He gave Adam and Eve free will to choose, He allowed them to make their own decisions and did not interfere or force them to do His will. God will teach, lead and guide, but He will not force.

God is omnipresent, so He is always everywhere, and the serpent knew this. Eve allowed herself to be seduced by the idea of being like God and picked the fruit and ate it before offering it to her husband, Adam, who was with her. Although Eve had disobeyed God, it wasn't until Adam ate of the fruit that the damage was done to mankind, because God had made an agreement with Adam and not with Eve. The Adamic Covenant, as it is known, was this agreement and it was in place before Eve was created. Adam had a wonderful relationship with God until he made the informed decision to choose Eve over God, defying the one order they were given and choosing death over life.

FACT

It is widely believed that the fruit that Adam and Eve ate was an apple, but the Bible does not support this in any way; it gives no name or description to the fruit that Adam and Eve ate. I believe it was a fig, because immediately after they ate from the tree and realised they were naked, they covered themselves with fig leaves!

"And when the woman saw that the tree was good for food, and that it was delightful to look at, and a tree to be desired in order to make one wise and insightful, she took some of its fruit and ate it; and she also gave some to her husband with her, and he ate. Then the eyes of the two of them were opened [that is, their awareness increased], and they knew that they were naked; and they fastened fig leaves together and made themselves coverings."

[Genesis 3:7 AMP]

Using excuses as a defence to justify your choices does not work with God. He will come to you directly to ensure you answer for your actions. God went directly to Adam, even though He knew what the serpent and Eve had done. What would have happened if only Eve had eaten of the fruit and Adam had resisted and remained obedient to God, we will never know. God does, however, acknowledge that Satan interfered with our destiny and that is why He put a plan in place to send His Son, Jesus, to help us by reversing the damage that was done to us. He did not leave us to be condemned for all eternity in our sin.

The moment Adam broke the agreement that God had made with him, sin entered the world. There is disease, sickness and death; the animals are no longer subject to us but instead we fear them. Everything was turned upside down and we now live in a 'broken world'. God had to kill an innocent animal for Adam and Eve to use the skin as clothing, as their innocence was gone and they were no longer covered in His glory.

The devil, yet again not thinking things through because of his pride, believed he could destroy something he did not create. He did not know that he could not separate us from God's love and that God, knowing this would happen, had already devised a plan—"The Plan of Redemption". Jesus would be born as a man, suffer and die to bring us back into a relationship with God, a chance Satan will never have again.

Through Jesus Christ we can be forgiven, much to Satan's dismay. I'm sure one of the questions you are asking yourself at this point is, "If God is all-powerful and ever-present, and if He could see that all this was going to happen, why didn't He stop it before it happened? Or why did He even create us in the first place?" Good question! I have asked myself the same thing.

To answer, I will break the golden rule of 'don't answer a question with a question' and you can decide on the answer for yourself. If you had unparalleled power, the ability to create things and to speak them into being, knew everything that would happen before it did and could be in all places at the same time, would you live a life doing nothing, not bothering to create, not bothering to do anything, but allowing yourself to simply 'sit through' all eternity? Or would you do what is in your nature to do, to create and to love and put any necessary plans in place for when mishaps and challenges occur and to have a great existence? I think you have your answer. God is the creator and He creates; He is love and He loves. His world is amazing whether we are in it or not, but our world is amazing only when He is in it.

Asking God questions is good, but trying to tell Him He should have done it this way, not that way, is not just futile but insulting. One lesson it is worth learning very early in your Christian life is to use the gifts that God has given you, but use them wisely and learn to deal with the interference of Satan, because he can't help himself. Be imitators of God, switch up the plan on Satan, strategise; he can't keep up, he can only guess. When God sent Jesus to us, the enemy had no idea what he was dealing with and God switched up the plan on him. Do not compare yourself and your ways to God's and think that because you would do it this way or that way, then God should do so also.

God's thoughts and ways go beyond ours. We do not think like Him and we certainly don't act like Him.

"'For My thoughts are not your thoughts, nor are your ways My ways,' declares the Lord."

[Isaiah 55:8 AMP]

We must learn to trust God completely, even when we do not fully understand His plans. That is true faith, as you will learn later. It's likely that God had a plan in place even before Adam and Eve had sinned, as the moment mankind fell, God revealed His plan to recover the situation. He didn't need to go away, give it some thought, then come back. God is always prepared, so we too should be prepared for the unexpected.

Redemption is the act of saving one from sin, error or evil. Through this plan God was able to regain possession, or to buy something back (man) in exchange for payment (Jesus), who paid the debt that we owed (death, the payment for sin). The following scripture tells of the fall of mankind and the prophecy of Christ suffering at the Cross for what we did:

"And I will put enmity [open hostility]
Between you and the woman,
And between your seed [offspring] and her Seed;
He shall [fatally] bruise your head,
And you shall [only] bruise His heel."

[Genesis 3:15 AMP]

Here God is speaking directly to Satan. God is saying there will now always be hostility between us and Satan, between mankind and Satan's kind, and we will not willingly see him as a friend or be taken in by him so easily again. The seed of the woman is Christ when He comes, and the seed of Satan is all things evil (sin).

The result of this antagonism is that Jesus will be victorious over him by bruising his head, taking away his power and his hold on mankind but not killing him, while Satan is only capable of bruising Jesus' heel, which represents Christ's suffering and death at the Cross. I would rather get a bruised heel than a kick in the head; the body can recover and exist with a damaged heel but it cannot exist without the head, so this is a symbolic representation of Satan's future. Even then Satan didn't 'get it' and he still thought he could compete with God! The only person who could bring us back into a relationship with God was His Son, Jesus Christ.

Recommended Reading

Genesis Chapters 1 and 2	The History of Creation
	The Garden of Eden
Genesis Chapter 3	The Fall of Mankind

ACTIVITY 1

Who is God? ....

....

What is Jesus' last name?...

....

Why can the world not accept the Holy Spirit?................................

....

Why did Adam call Eve 'woman'? ....

....

What was the plan of Redemption designed to do?............................

....

....

Which tree was located next to the tree of the knowledge of good
and evil? ....

....

Notes: ....

....

....

....

....

....

....

....

God Is Here

In the beginning we were created
Perfect in all our ways, innocent as newborn babes
But deceit, deception and dangerous liaisons
Brought about such a cataclysmic reaction
One thing led to another
Pain and estrangement from our Father
The world turned upside down
And into turmoil we were thrown.

Expelled in shame and grace
That was the punishment to the human race
Out of the presence of God our Father
Distance growing ever farther
The 'knowledge' of good and evil we desired
Became but a curse as it transpired
To be like God, in our vain pursuit
Snatched from His glory and left destitute.

But His love knew no bound
And mercy in His sight we found
His one and only Son He sent
To tell us our sentence was spent
For He countered the attack on our race
Bringing us back under grace
So now we have hope in Christ
For no one else could pay that price.

Our aim, to be one again with God
But to be with our Father, we must go through His Son
The journey is long with challenges along the way
Now there is nothing for us to pay
Revealing all through His Holy Spirit
Protection from Satan who dropped us in it!
Many kick against the prick and jeer
But I'm so glad GOD that You are here.

CHAPTER 2
THE JOURNEY OF FAITH

"Jesus replied, 'Have faith in God [constantly]. I assure you and most solemnly say to you, whoever says to this mountain, "Be lifted up and thrown into the sea!" and does not doubt in his heart [in God's unlimited power], but believes that what he says is going to take place, it will be done for him [in accordance with God's will].'"

Mark 11:22-23 AMP

Christianity is the belief in Jesus Christ, that He is the Son of the living God, that He came to die for the sins of the world, and that He will one day return to reward His followers and judge the rest of the world.

"Christ died for our sins according to [that which] the Scriptures [foretold], and that He was buried, and that He was [bodily] raised on the third day according to [that which] the Scriptures [foretold]."

[1 Corinthians 15:3-4 AMP]

To be a Christian is to be like Christ, to be 'imitators of Christ', to live as He did, to love as He did. Christianity is the world's largest faith with over two billion Christians worldwide (source: www.pewresearch.org). Christianity was born out of the death and resurrection (reawakening, rebirth) of Jesus Christ. The following scripture tells us what God did for us and why He did it:

"For God so loved the world that He gave his only begotten Son, that whosoever believes in Him should not perish, but have everlasting life."

[John 3:16]

Jesus had to counteract the damage that Satan did in order to bring us back into a relationship with God. What He did birthed

Christianity. The first four books of the New Testament (Matthew, Mark, Luke and John, known as the Gospels, meaning 'the good news') tell us about Jesus' birth, death and resurrection in detail. Christianity is often referred to as a religion, but it is not a religion; it is a real relationship with the real God, it is a faith. Everything Jesus did on Earth was by faith—the miracles, the healings, the pain and suffering, the ultimate trust in God to lay down His life and pick it up again.

Often people will say "you're religious", but the reality is no, you're not religious, because you have a real relationship with God. The Christian's belief is not in a set of man-made religious rules but in God, His love and His teachings, and is strengthened by nurturing a real relationship with Him. This concept is not an easy one to understand as religion and faith are used interchangeably.

Faith is a *complete* trust or confidence in someone, based on spiritual conviction. It is a different belief system from that of believing in each other, the limited abilities of human beings, superhuman beings, manmade images, inanimate objects or animals. A Christian's faith lies in Jesus Christ and His work when He came and died for us, which brought us back into a relationship with God the Father through His Holy Spirit. Faith should grow throughout the life of a Christian as they understand who they are in Christ and allow the Holy Spirit to teach and guide them to all truths. When life is good and everything is going well it is easy for your faith to grow, but there will be times when things are not going so well, and your faith can be weakened. It is at this time that many people look for something else to put their faith in and often end up confused and caught up in religious groups and practices. When we have faith in God, we live with complete hope and expectation in Him and Him alone.

"Now faith is the assurance [title deed, confirmation] of things hoped for [divinely guaranteed], and the evidence of things not seen [the conviction of their reality—faith comprehends as fact what cannot be experienced by the physical senses]. For by this [kind of] faith the men of old gained [divine] approval.

By faith [that is, with an inherent trust and enduring confidence in the power, wisdom and goodness of God] we understand that the worlds [universe, ages] were framed and created [formed, put in order, and equipped for their intended purpose] by the word of God, so that what is seen was not made out of things which are visible."

[Hebrews 11:1-3 AMP]

Faith teaches us to see not just with our physical eyes but also with our spiritual eyes. Before God created the world, it was void and in darkness; then something was formed out of something that was not visible. The world was spoken into being, and the foundation of our faith rests on this belief. Paul teaches that "the just shall live by faith" [Romans 1:17 NKJV] in God, and that we should avoid religious practices.

"Therefore let no one judge you in regard to food and drink or in regard to [the observance of] a festival or a new moon or a Sabbath day. Such things are only a shadow of what is to come and they have only symbolic value; but the substance [the reality of what is foreshadowed] belongs to Christ. Let no one defraud you of your prize [your freedom in Christ and your salvation] by insisting on mock humility and the worship of angels, going into detail about visions [he claims] he has seen [to justify his authority], puffed up [in conceit] by his unspiritual mind…"

[Colossians 2:16-18 AMP]

Attempting to worship God by a set of religious rules is not faith in God. The eating or drinking of specific foods and drink, celebrating religious festivals or Sabbaths, deceiving others and pretending to be humble or modest are prideful and vain pursuits, as is the worship of angels.

Everyone has faith to some degree and a belief in something or someone; it is an innate attribute in us. People have faith in each other, their spouses, their relationships, their jobs, their own abilities, or their ideal life, and when something happens to upset that belief system, their faith is weakened, and they are left confused.

Religion

Adhering to religion and religious practices demonstrates belief in and worship of a superhuman controlling power, especially (but not always) a personal God. Much of this belief has been dictated by traditions, cultures, habits, vain desires and power-seekers with the need to control.

Being religious and being faithful are worlds apart. Religion and religious practices encourage people to depend on their own works, strength and ability to succeed. Religion says, 'I must go to church every Sunday to be holy, because if I don't people will think I'm not a Christian.' In this example, your faith lies in people and what they think of you and not in Christ. Your reason for going to church becomes rooted in pleasing man and not in pleasing God. Faith on the other hand says, 'Going to church every Sunday does not make you a Christian. If you can't make it to church sometimes, God will not hold it against you.' You go to church because you choose to; you love God and you want to worship Him of your own free will, not because you feel pressured.

Religion says, 'I must pray for several hours each day and at the same time, otherwise I won't get into heaven.' Whilst praying is a must for the Christian, trying to put yourself under a regime and having faith in your ability to follow the set of rules you have inflicted on yourself will ultimately lead to self-condemnation when you fail. Again, your faith is in yourself and your ability and not in Christ.

'I must look a certain way and cannot wear this or that and can't do my hair in this style or that style and must cover my face'— more man-made religious practices. God did not ask this of us. His Holy Spirit works with us to help us to dress and look a way that is becoming of a Christian. God deals with our hearts and not our looks. Many things that society dictates, which many religions profess to be true, you will not find in the Holy Bible.

There are many laws and practices in the Old Testament that the Lord no longer expects us to live by because mankind was not able to live by them during the time of the Old Testament and is still not able to do so now. For this reason, God sent His Holy Spirit to help us to live a holy life by depending on His strength and not ours. This issue continues to be a source of much confusion for new and mature Christians alike. Whilst God has a clear set of rules and guidelines to enable us to live righteous lives, He does not try to make our lives miserable by de-humanising us and making us suffer. Misery, self-condemnation, guilt, failure, judging or being judged by others and persecution are not of God. Religious practices are damaging and are prevalent when there is little or no faith in the one true God. It causes confusion and ultimately people end up rejecting God and blaming Him for everything that goes wrong in their lives.

Religion actually pulls the believer away from Christ, away from their spirituality, and draws them towards self-righteousness. To avoid this, we must study the Word of God and live according to His ways. If you don't know God or His teachings, you will struggle to know whether you are being taught true Bible doctrine. How can you challenge a lie if you don't know what the truth is?

Hope

Knowing the truth is a must. A lack of knowledge of your faith can have unexpected consequences. As a result of this many Christians have become disillusioned, whilst others are confused by the teachings and ultimately walk away from them, looking for hope in something else. Many become disgruntled or emotionally bruised, finding themselves going back to living without hope, living without Christ. One comment I heard from a new Christian within months of her coming to the faith was, "I don't know if this Christian life is really for me. What is it all about anyway? I'm more confused now than before I started out."

Deeply saddened to hear this, I sat listening to her concerns. Through further discussions I found out that she was feeling very lonely, didn't feel a part of the church community and didn't understand what 'it' was all about. No one was spending quality time with her to help her through her first experiences—the baby stage.

Life is a journey of choices. We are born, we live and we die. These are *the* facts of life. The journey, however, is different for everyone, and how we live and die matters, as this defines our eternal destination. Christianity is a journey unlike any other. You are travelling with God, whom you cannot see but you know is there. You must learn to speak to Him and hear Him when He speaks to you. God will teach you about the kingdom of heaven, the spiritual world and how our physical world is affected and controlled by it. On your journey you will learn not to rely on your own understanding but to rely on God's understanding.

Christianity teaches that the struggles in life, the battles, are all spiritual and against powers that we have no understanding of. If we don't know or understand the enemy, we cannot fight the battle. We will have no strategy in place and will not be using the right weapons. A physical war requires physical weapons, so a spiritual war requires spiritual weapons. The following scripture gives us an insight into the enemy we are wrestling against:

"For our struggle is not against flesh and blood [contending only with physical opponents], but against the rulers, against the powers, against the world forces of this [present] darkness, against the spiritual forces of wickedness in the heavenly [supernatural] places."

[Ephesians 6:12 AMP]

It is not what you can see that you should be cautious of, it is what you cannot see; but you will have a part to play. What you really need to remember from the outset is that, although you meet and interact with others along the way, this journey is between you and God. Others can help and encourage you, harm you even, but ultimately it is all about your personal relationship with God. You and you alone are responsible for your journey with Christ. This journey is offered to everyone and not just a chosen few, for in God's eyes no one is more worthy than another.

FACT

Christianity is available to everyone, without exception. Regardless of what you have done, or the type of life you have led, forgiveness (compassion, mercy) and salvation (deliverance, rescue) is for you. It is confirmed by Peter in the book of Acts:

"And it shall be that everyone who calls upon the name of the Lord [invoking, adoring, and worshiping the Lord Jesus] shall be saved [rescued spiritually]."

[Acts 2:21 AMP]

If you think you have done something so wrong that God couldn't possibly love you or forgive you, let me be the first to tell you that this is not true. Christ died for absolutely *everyone*. There are so many false doctrines in the world today claiming that God will not forgive you if you've done this or you will be going to hell because you've done that. My only answer to that is:

"Do not judge and criticise and condemn [others unfairly with an attitude of self-righteous superiority as though assuming the office of a judge], so that you will not be judged [unfairly]. For just as you [hypocritically] judge others [when you are sinful and unrepentant], so will you be judged; and in accordance with your standard of measure [used to pass out judgment], judgment will be measured to you. Why do you look at the [insignificant] speck that is in your brother's eye, but do not notice and acknowledge the [egregious] log that is in your own eye?"

[Matthew 7:1-3 AMP]

We must never pass judgement on others, as we don't have that right; we should not tell them what we think their ultimate fate will be, because we do not know. Only Jesus has the right to judge, and it will not be done in this age. It is only when this world as we know it has ended and the judgement age begins that those who rejected the Lord will be judged.

There seem to be many prophecies, with many people claiming they have received a message from God, that He will be bringing judgement to a country or to a particular group of people. God is blamed for just about everything bad that happens in the world today. The very idea that God is pronouncing judgement on people in this Age of Grace is fundamentally wrong and no Christian should be perpetuating those beliefs. This is an incorrect representation of God—this is not the judgement age. This is the age of second chances, love, forgiveness and blessings. Jesus came to save and not to judge, so anything that is happening in this age— natural disasters, excessive loss of life—is not God judging anyone, but a fallen world continually breaking apart.

Christians who claim that God is killing people to judge them for their wickedness are encouraging the world to hate God and to blame Him for all the bad things that happen to their loved ones.

These teachings give people a reason not to accept Jesus as their Lord and Saviour, preventing them from knowing the truth and accepting salvation. This is the time for telling people about the love of God and His saving grace and what they need to do to enter the kingdom of heaven.

Satan has many strategies in place to deceive people. He will use even the people who claim to love God, if they let him. He continues to manipulate generations into thinking that they are too evil for God to forgive them. These are the same subtle tactics Satan used to convince Adam and Eve to be disobedient to God, but they still had a choice, as do we. Unless we begin to understand the spiritual world that we live in, and how to strategise, he will continue manipulating us unchecked. If he can convince you that you are not worthy of forgiveness, you won't ask for it and will remain in sin, but you do have a choice. Jesus came to save *you,* so don't let His sacrifice be in vain. But who is Jesus and what did He do?

Recommended Reading

Hebrews Chapter 11	The Foundation of Faith
1 Corinthians Chapter 15	Faith in the Risen Christ

ACTIVITY 2

What is the difference between faith and religion? ....

....

....

Who is Jesus? ....

....

We all have faith. True or False?...

....

Explain the previous statement:...

....

....

Why did God give His only Son to die for us? ....

....

....

Jesus is just for Christians. True or False? ....

....

Notes: ....

CHAPTER 3
JESUS IS MORE THAN...

A man, a carpenter, a fisherman, a teacher, an historical figure, a prophet or any other title that the world chooses to give Him. To many He was born, He preached and taught, was a radical, and was eventually crucified and died. That is where it ends for most people, but for the Christian that is just the beginning, because we know Jesus rose again. So, where does this Christian journey start? How can you join and where does it end? The simple answer is: it starts with Jesus, joining is free and easy, and it ends with Jesus.

The world generally accepts that Jesus existed, as there are historical records to prove this, but any true Christian will tell you that Jesus is more than the title assigned to Him by a race—the human race, that does not know where they came from, why they are here or where they are going. Jesus is our Saviour; He is God with us!

"'She will give birth to a Son, and you shall name Him Jesus [The Lord is salvation], for He will save His people from their sins.' All this happened in order to fulfil what the Lord had spoken through the prophet [Isaiah]: 'Behold, the virgin shall be with child and give birth to a Son, and they shall call His name Immanuel'—which, when translated, means, 'God with us.'"

[Matthew 1:21-23 AMP]

Though there are people who do not believe that Jesus is the Son of God, this does not mean it is not so. Jesus was born to Mary, an earthly mother and a virgin, but He was not conceived by Joseph, His earthly father. If He had been conceived by an earthly father, He would have been born in sin and corrupted by it like the rest of us. An unclean vessel cannot cleanse an unclean vessel; neither can be of benefit to the other. Jesus was born of the Holy Spirit.

"Joseph, descendant of David, do not be afraid to take Mary as your wife, for the Child who has been conceived in her is of the Holy Spirit."

[Matthew 1:20 AMP]

Joseph was engaged to Mary and, knowing she was pregnant, considered ways to send her away discreetly to hide her shame so she would not be humiliated or stoned. But God sent an angel to him to explain that she had not been unfaithful, and that her pregnancy was the work of the Holy Spirit. God alerted the world to this amazing event by placing a star in the sky for astrologers and wise men who read the stars to see and follow to Jesus' birthplace, in order to pay homage to and revere His Son.

FACT

The Bible does not state how many wise men came to see Jesus after He was born. Through time and errors, we have been led to believe it was three. This number was possibly arrived at because the gifts mentioned were Gold, Frankincense and Myrrh—three gifts, three men! Not so. These were the gifts given to kings at that time.

Ask yourself this: would there really only have been three wise men and astrologers on the Earth at that time studying the stars? An event so great would have attracted huge speculation; the news would have been spread far and wide. King Herod's attention would not have been drawn to three men covertly travelling across the desert, and we know God did not hide the birth of His Son. The birth of Jesus had been prophesied throughout the Old Testament and John the Baptist preached on it daily in the New Testament, so much so that they beheaded him for it.

Jesus was born in Bethlehem of Judea and His birth was no mean feat. God protected Him all the way, while the angels of heaven would have been on high alert. I imagine Michael and the warrior angels were very busy fighting many spiritual battles during this time, along with Gabriel and the messenger angels delivering messages in the heavens and on the Earth. There is so much more that we have not been privy to. Satan and his followers were trying very hard to prevent Jesus' birth, but we know he could not and did not succeed.

Jesus' Public Ministry

Jesus started His public ministry at the age of thirty. He died and rose again three and a half years later. Not much is written about our Lord up to Him starting His public ministry, because God the Father gave Him time to experience life as a human being in order to understand our struggles, challenges and emotions and prepare for His journey ahead. We have a limitless God who existed before time began. He is awesome in greatness and power and decided to put Himself into a limited body to feel pain, hunger and suffering, refusing to use His infinite power to avoid it. That adjustment would have taken some doing.

Jesus lived as normal a life as possible until He performed His first miracle, which was turning water into wine. He attended a wedding and they ran out of wine, so Jesus instructed the servants to fill the waterpots with water and, when the water was poured and given to the guests, it was wine. But this wine tasted much better than the wine they'd been drinking up to that point.

"Jesus said to the servants, 'Fill the waterpots with water.' So they filled them up to the brim. Then He said to them, 'Draw some out now and take it to the headwaiter [of the banquet].' So they took it to him. And when the headwaiter tasted the water which had turned into wine, not knowing where it came from (though the servants who had drawn the water knew) he called the bridegroom, and said to him, 'Everyone else serves his best wine first, and when people have drunk freely, then he serves that which is not so good; but you have kept back the good wine until now.'"

[John 2:7-10 AMP]

The two things that most people struggle with are that Jesus is the 'Son of God' and that He performed 'miracles'. There is so much to learn about our Lord that we cannot even begin to scratch the surface in these few pages. The Bible itself could not contain all the great things Jesus did when He was on this Earth. That is why the best starting point when reading and studying the Bible is Jesus. You could spend your whole Christian life learning about the Lord and never exhaust the topic; there is always something more to learn and understand.

Discussing our Lord Jesus is a good thing and is to be encouraged. However, there are some discussions which are meaningless and serve no purpose other than to anger the participants. One such discussion, which continues to be a 'bone of contention', is Jesus' colour. Was He black, or white with blonde hair and blue eyes? Whilst there is nothing wrong with the question, I have witnessed people getting angry during these discussions when someone disagrees with their point of view and refuses to accept their version of the truth. Jesus was not black; He was also not white. He was not from Ethiopia, Europe, Africa, China or India. He was born in Bethlehem. He was a Jew. If we use these simple facts and let common sense prevail, then He was of the same colour as the people from that part of the world, whether it was two thousand years ago or not.

The many images we see of Jesus through the ages have been personal representations from individuals and, whilst it is good that every race wants to claim Him, these images should not be seen as accurate or factual representations of what He looked like and, of course, it shouldn't matter. All the arguments with one race claiming He had their skin colour and others not wanting to worship Him because of it—some people even find pictures of earthly men and claim He looked like them—are redundant! Please don't get caught up with these useless discussions as they serve no purpose at all.

If you are still not happy with this simple but truthful explanation, ask yourself these questions: how does Jesus' colour in any way affect what He did for mankind? Does the colour of Jesus' skin have anything to do with the fact that we can only be saved through Him? If your answer is 'yes, if He was white I wouldn't have anything to do with Him' or 'if He was black I wouldn't have anything to do with Him', then you definitely need Him. The colour of His skin is not important, only what He did for mankind!

Jesus did many things to show the wonders of God's kingdom and still people refused to believe in Him. He did not raise the dead in secret, He did it publicly. He healed the sick publicly, He taught in the synagogues, and thousands followed Him and listened to His preaching and teaching, but He was still rejected. There is no one else in the history of the world who has had this level of impact on people's lives—no king, no ruler, no celebrity. No one!

Therefore, no matter how much proof God provides for the world, with all the signs and wonders that He displays, if people have made up their minds not to accept something, they won't. Jesus' purpose was to reverse the damage Adam did to mankind. He came to bless us and remove the curse, and He did this regardless of whether the human race accepted Him or not. Adam was born naked, innocent and knew no shame; but by the time he, Satan and Eve had finished, all this was reversed. When they sinned and mankind became cursed, they had to be covered inadequately with the skin of innocent animals to cover their shame.

Jesus was born and clothed with the inadequate clothing of mankind and had to endure shame and humiliation to have the inadequate covering stripped away. He was stripped naked to be covered once again in the innocence that was lost in the Garden of Eden. Jesus came to tell us of the kingdom of heaven, how much God loves us and what we need to do to find Him again. For this to happen, He had to die. His pure, uncorrupted, innocent blood had to be shed to protect us from the power of Satan so that we would have free access to God once more, rendering Satan ineffective at the same time—though not powerless. When God looks at us now, He no longer sees our sin; He sees the holy covering that is the blood of His Son Jesus.

Why Death?

But 'Why death?' you ask. Why did Jesus have to die, and why this emphasis on blood being shed? The blood of a human being is the life force of the person. Before Adam sinned, we had life in God's presence, death was not in the plan, and blood had never been shed from us or any animal. When Adam sinned, the punishment was death, but not immediately. His spiritual death was immediate but physical death came later. However, death entered the animal kingdom and the world immediately as God had to kill an innocent animal to cover man with the skin.

"The Lord God made tunics of [animal] skins for Adam and his wife and clothed them."

[Genesis 3:21 AMP]

Jesus had to come to Earth to bring spiritual life back to mankind, and He had to die because only His blood is innocent and could protect us again spiritually. Just as the innocent blood of the animal represented a physical and inadequate covering for mankind, the innocent blood of Jesus represents a complete spiritual covering for us. God tells us very clearly in the scriptures that the blood in a living being is the life of that person or animal and, in the case of animals, we should not eat it with the meat.

"Only be sure that you do not eat the blood, for the blood is the life [soul], and you shall not eat the life with the meat. You shall not eat it; you shall pour it out on the ground like water."

[Deuteronomy 12:23-24 AMP]

The difference between our blood and Jesus' blood is that our blood gives life to our individual bodies, but Jesus' blood gives life to mankind. He is the source of our life, so, in dying and shedding His blood, He gave us life eternal. He fulfilled the scriptures and the prophecies written about Him throughout the Bible, which is God's Word and perfect will. It is for this reason that Jesus is called the Word of God, because He is the perfect will of God in the flesh. He removed the great divide between God and us.

The blood of Jesus gives us access to eternal life with Him. The Cross represents all these things to a Christian. Often you will hear Christians say, 'we are grateful for what Christ did on the Cross' or, 'our faith lies in the Cross', or you will hear teachings on the 'Cross'. It is all about the sacrifice Christ made by dying on the Cross, which means everything to a Christian; it is the foundation of our faith.

Jesus had to bring the flesh, meaning the natural man and his will, under the control of the Spirit. As physical beings born in sin, our flesh is constantly fighting against our spirit. Adam represents the flesh will of man, whilst Jesus is the spirit of man; Adam was born of the flesh and Jesus was born of the Spirit.

"So it is written [in Scripture], 'The first man, Adam, became a living soul [an individual]; the last Adam [Christ] became a life-giving spirit [restoring the dead to life]. However, the spiritual [the immortal life] is not first, but the physical [the mortal life]; then the spiritual. The first man [Adam] is from the earth, earthy [made of dust]; the second Man [Christ, the Lord] is from heaven. As is the earthly man [the man of dust], so are those who are of earth; and as is the heavenly [Man], so are those who are of heaven. Just as we have borne the image of the earthly [the man of dust], we will also bear the image of the heavenly [the Man of heaven]."

[1 Corinthians 15:45-49 AMP]

The flesh and the natural man came first, from the earth, and the spiritual man came second, from heaven. The flesh will always fight against the spirit, and this struggle will remain with us throughout our lives. The Holy Spirit works with our spirit to bring us to a place of righteousness (holy and upright living according to God's standard) in Christ; but the more we live in the spirit—which is to allow the Holy Spirit to work with us, sanctify (cleanse and purify) us and lead us—and study and live by the Bible's teachings, the flesh will become more subdued and the spirit will become more dominant in our lives. When Jesus died on the Cross, the flesh would have been fighting not to be put through that pain, not to have to suffer like that, and the Holy Spirit would have been very active in strengthening His spirit so He could go through it. So we see here, at the crucifixion of Christ, the perfect dominance of the spirit over the flesh.

Throughout Jesus' life He led by example. He was baptised by John the Baptist (not the disciple John who later became an Apostle), which was witnessed by God the Father and God the Holy Spirit. The moment He received His water baptism from John, He was filled with the Holy Spirit, who drove Him straight up into the wilderness where He fasted for forty days and nights and was tempted by the devil. This is the same path for every new Christian. The devil will be on your case tempting and trying to deceive you into giving up your inheritance from the moment you make that commitment to follow Christ, so it is important for you to let the Holy Spirit guide you. The battle is real—don't let anyone convince you otherwise.

Jesus needed to train others to take over His work when He returned to heaven, so He recruited twelve disciples (followers, believers). These were not chosen by chance. God had already chosen them for Jesus and, when He saw them, He called them to Him. In Matthew 17, Jesus prays for His disciples, confirming that they were chosen by God the Father. Jesus spent many hours praying to His Father away from the public. He knew His purpose on Earth and He did not depart from it. Although He and John the Baptist were cousins, they didn't take 'time out' to visit each other and have great family reunions (not that there is anything wrong with family reunions!) but they remained completely focused on the task ahead.

Distractions

Often on our Christian journey we get distracted by the things of the world and go off track, but it is very important to remain focused. This is not to say you cannot enjoy time with family and friends, but when we lose focus and come off track without realising, it can be difficult to get back on the right path. John the Baptist and Jesus both knew their purposes and they fulfilled them without deviating. Just as we are determined and single-minded when we want to achieve something in life—studying for a degree, preparing for that all-important new career, planning and saving for a new home—so too must the commitment to your Christian life be. Put God first!

Jesus spent a lot of time with the twelve disciples, teaching them and revealing things to them so that they could carry on His work once He had gone back up to heaven. They in turn would build the church and teach others, and the work would continue from generation to generation. And here we are, approximately two thousand years later, continuing on that journey. The disciples were Jesus' inner circle; they lived, worked and experienced life together for the best part of three years.

Their purpose was not only to preach the kingdom of heaven to this world, but they have a purpose in the next world as well. Peter asked the Lord what their reward would be for leaving family and home and following Him.

"Jesus said to them, 'I assure you and most solemnly say to you, in the renewal [that is, the Messianic restoration and regeneration of all things] when the Son of Man sits on His glorious throne, you [who have followed Me, becoming My disciples] will also sit on twelve thrones, judging the twelve tribes of Israel.'"

[Matthew 19:28 AMP]

So the disciples' purpose was to preach and teach the world about Jesus and the kingdom of heaven and build the church. They would then ultimately become judges over the twelve tribes of Israel on the day of judgement. That is true fulfilment of purpose both in this life and beyond. You too have a purpose to fulfil in Jesus Christ. Knowing that purpose is half the story, and fulfilling it is the other; but we must strive to find out what our purpose is, and persevere to fulfilment. We will address this later in the book.

Jesus preached and taught wherever He went. He healed the sick, raised the dead and performed miracles, so much so that a lot of people didn't want to hear about the kingdom of heaven and being saved; they wanted to see the miracles and to be healed from their diseases.

It is very important for you to understand something here. The world is diseased with sin, and the by-products of sin are death, sickness, hatred, evil and <u>all</u> manner of wrongdoings. Jesus came to eradicate the disease, the root cause, which is sin. He didn't come to nurse the symptoms, He came to break the power of sin over our lives and to replace that with salvation and eternal life. The miracles and the wonders followed Jesus because of who He was and the power He had. By focusing on doing the will of the Father, the blessings and the power followed Jesus wherever He went. Due to His very nature—holiness, virtue, love and compassion—sin could not endure when it came into contact with Him. His love and compassion were so great that all who were sick with diverse diseases were healed when they touched Him or when He touched them. Many were also healed without Him touching them; He could simply command their healing and they were healed. Demons had to flee as they could not remain in His presence.

Many Christians become very desperate for the miracles and start chasing signs and wonders, shifting their focus from the will of God, which is to spread the gospel about His Son and His kingdom to the corners of the earth. When the focus shifts from Jesus and we make the miracles our central focus, we can become ineffective, making our Christianity work-based and not faith-based. The focus has to be Jesus. When we chase after Him and are single-mindedly driven to spreading the gospel, guess what? The blessings and the miracles and the power will follow you and you cannot help but heal the sick, cast out demons and work miracles just as Jesus did. And here is the proof:

"And He said to them, 'Go into all the world and preach the gospel to every creature. He who believes and is baptised will be saved; but he who does not believe will be condemned. And these signs will follow those who believe: In My name they will cast out demons; they will speak with new tongues; they will take up serpents; and if they drink anything deadly, it will by no means hurt them; they will lay hands on the sick, and they will recover.'"

[Mark 16:15-18 NKJV]

Studying the Bible and living by it, allowing it to saturate your spirit and allowing the Holy Spirit to be active in your life, are the building blocks of your Christian faith. Without doing this you are still at the starting block. When your focus shifts, it is usually replaced by religious practices, false doctrines, and seductive and enticing New Wave teachings that sound good to the untrained mind. But it is not by our power or our might that signs and wonders happen, it is by the power of the Holy Spirit of God:

"'Not by might nor by power, but by My Spirit,'
Says the Lord of hosts."

[Zechariah 4:6 NKJV]

When our loved ones are sick or dying, we want them to be healed and we pray frantically for them not to die. Jesus' purpose was not to prolong this life, but to help us live it the right way. Our primary aim is to tell our loved ones about Him and help them to deal with the pain and suffering of this world, knowing that there is something better waiting for them when this life is over.

Although Jesus did so much and saved so many people before He died, many walked away from Him because they didn't understand His teachings and so became fearful. Even when He cast out legions of demons from two men living in caves and terrifying the inhabitants, the people were themselves so scared that instead of wanting the Lord to remain with them, they asked Him to leave [Matthew 8:28-33]. Fear makes people do cruel things to each other. Unfortunately, this is the world we live in.

Persecutions

Jesus experienced rejection, betrayal and pain. He was lied about, plotted against and had His character sullied. He was challenged at every turn but He was truly innocent of all charges. When we make a commitment to follow Christ, we too will experience some of the challenges He went through; some for the faith and some in life in general. Being persecuted for your faith is a real possibility.

FACT

Jesus confirms that the journey will be difficult. When people don't understand you, they will alienate and victimise you. They will know there is something different about you, but won't be able to quite put their finger on it. So as a consequence, they may reject you.

"If the world hates you [and it does], know that it has hated Me before it hated you. If you belonged to the world, the world would love [you as] its own and would treat you with affection. But you are not of the world [you no longer belong to it], but I have chosen you out of the world. And because of this the world hates you. Remember [and continue to remember] that I told you, 'A servant is not greater than his master.' If they persecuted Me, they will also persecute you. If they kept My word, they will keep yours also."

[John 15:18-20 AMP]

As I write these words, Christians are being persecuted and killed in many parts of the world for their faith, so we must expect the unexpected at all times and be prepared for it. In this age, defending your faith is the reality and not the exception, so the Lord is telling us here that it won't be easy. His own people hated Him, so our own will hate us too. The very people you love and trust may let you down, but you must know who you serve and, no matter how difficult the journey gets, you must endure to the end. Even if you have to crawl over the finish line, make sure you get there.

A word of caution, though. Though we are no longer of the world, please do not think we are better than anyone else in the world, because we are not. We do not place ourselves on pedestals, because there is only one way off those; we do not look down on others and we do not treat anyone as any less than ourselves. As Christians we do not condone people's sin but must love the person regardless without judging them. Sometimes people will say you are judging them even when you are not. Identifying when something is wrong, which we should do, is not judging a person. Stating a fact about something that someone may be doing is not judging them. Judging is when you have decided to pass a sentence on the person because of their current actions.

You will find that, more often than not, it is the world that will judge you as a Christian. People often decide that you are going to judge them, so they become hostile towards you in anticipation.

Jesus did not come to judge. He came to bless us through His sacrifice, and this shows the extent of God's love for us. We in turn must show love to each other regardless of what we are going through. Jesus' suffering surpasses anything that anyone could ever experience in their whole life. He knew what would happen to Him and still went through with it. Imagine knowing that you are going to die in such a brutal way and seeing it before it happens! Could you exercise the ultimate restraint, knowing you have the power to stop it, but you don't? Instead, you continue with your mission, fulfilling your promise to a people who will reject you even beyond the grave!

The extent of Jesus' very real pain is felt in the Garden of Gethsemane (meaning oil press), the night before the crucifixion. He wept and His sweat was like drops of blood as it fell from Him. "And He withdrew from them about a stone's throw, and knelt down and prayed, saying, 'Father, if You are willing, remove this cup [of divine wrath] from Me; yet not My will, but [always] Yours be done.' Now an angel appeared to Him from heaven, strengthening Him. And being in agony [deeply distressed and anguished, almost to the point of death], He prayed more intently; and His sweat became like drops of blood, falling down on the ground."

[Luke 22:41-44 AMP]

Jesus prayed to the Father to ask if it was possible not to have to endure the inevitable. Jesus would have seen that they would spit in His face, accuse Him of all manner of evils, tell lies about Him, mock Him, beat Him, pull out His beard, strip Him naked, whip Him, make Him carry His own cross, hammer nails into His hands and feet and give Him vinegar to drink; and they did! He saw all of this and still died on the Cross for us.

If at this point you are wondering what would have happened if Jesus had gone back up to heaven and decided not to go through with it, you are not the first and won't be the last. It made me shudder to think of it, so I've stopped wondering. The fact is that He did suffer and die for me and you; I love Him for it, and so should you.

Many Christians struggle on their journey when they come to the realisation that not all Christians will love and support them and that some will even hurt them. Remember, people are still human beings with wills of their own and no one is perfect, though we should strive for perfection. If we have taken a vow to follow Christ and we look at how He lived and died, it shouldn't be too difficult to see that we too will experience hurt and pain at the hands of both our own people and strangers.

After all, Jesus died at the hands of His own people: the Scribes, Pharisees, Sadducees, the Sanhedrin, temple elders and the Jewish people whom He grew up with. He taught them daily in the synagogues and healed them and their loved ones. The religious leaders knew who He was but pretended not to. They were scornful of Him because, as per their interpretation of the Old Testament prophecies, He should have been born as a worldly king in a palace and should have fought their battles in a way that they wanted to dictate. They refused to accept that a carpenter's son could be the Son of God and was in fact greater than them.

"The chief priests and the scribes were looking for a way to put Him to death; for they were afraid of the people [who listened devotedly to His teaching, and who respected His spiritual wisdom].

Then Satan entered Judas, the one called Iscariot, who was one of the twelve [disciples]. And he went away and discussed with the chief priests and officers how he might betray Him and hand Him over to them. They were delighted and agreed with him to give him money. So he consented, and began looking for a good opportunity to betray Jesus to them [at a time when He was] separated from the crowd [because the people might riot or stop them from seizing Him]."

[Luke 22:2-6 AMP]

So, we see that the very people who should have 'had His back' sought to destroy Him. He questioned them about it many times and tried to reason with them by pointing out what they were doing. But their hearts were stubborn, and they were relentless in their efforts to get rid of Him. The Jews were not allowed to put anyone to death, so they brought false accusations to the Roman leader—their enemy, Pontius Pilate—and pressured him to do it instead. The Romans had oppressed the Jews for many years, yet they were not the ones demanding Jesus' death. In fact, Pontius Pilate tried to release Jesus on more than one occasion.

"Pilate answered, 'I am not a Jew, am I? Your own people and their chief priests have handed You over to me. What have You done [that is worthy of death]?'"

[John 18:35 AMP]

And in verse 38, after questioning Jesus for some time, Pontius Pilate went out to the Jews and said, "I find no fault in Him at all." Now, let me take a moment to repeat two very important words here in case we miss the importance of this statement: Pilate found nothing "AT ALL". Not one single reason did he find to punish Jesus or put Him to death. His final attempt to release Jesus was in giving the Jews the choice to release the murderer Barabbas or Jesus, and the Jewish people (Jesus' people) chose a murderer over their Lord…and we think we have a lot to complain about when someone doesn't like us?

Regardless of what Jesus went through at the hands of the people who should have loved and cherished Him, He did not give up. No matter how great the injustice, we need to know how to stand up for what we believe in, how to go through the disappointments and the hurt and how to come out of every situation stronger than when we went in. A Christian must learn to use these experiences to spend time with the Lord and allow the Holy Spirit to make them stronger through it.

Judas Iscariot betrayed Jesus with a kiss; and did it break Him? Did it throw Him off track? No! Did Jesus hate him for it? No! Did Jesus blame God for picking Judas as one of the twelve disciples for

His Son? No! This is as good a time as any to reinforce the fact that we need to get over the things other people do to us and continue with the journey ahead.

"And Jesus said to him, 'Judas, are you betraying the Son of Man with a kiss?'"

[Luke 22:48 AMP]

The challenges are great whether we are betrayed by the people closest to us or by strangers, but people struggle the most when they are betrayed by someone they love and care about. Strangers owe us nothing, so we have no expectations of them; but we have expectations of our family, friends and other believers, so betrayal tends to be a stumbling block for many. Jesus took all that mankind gave Him and all that Satan could muster up and came out of it stronger than when He went in, and He still loves us!

"After this, Jesus, knowing that all was now finished, said in fulfilment of the Scripture, 'I am thirsty.' A jar full of sour wine was placed there; so they put a sponge soaked in the sour wine on [a branch of] hyssop and held it to His mouth. When Jesus had received the sour wine, He said, 'It is finished!' And He bowed His head and [voluntarily] gave up His spirit."

[John 19:28-30 AMP]

When Jesus died for us on the Cross, He did all that God had asked of Him to save mankind. Many people don't seem to really understand what this means for us. There is nothing else that God has to do to save us. There is no part two; there is certainly nothing that any man or woman can do to surpass that. All things have been fulfilled in Christ Jesus. Many false doctrines spring up today trying to create something new and trying to 'go beyond the Cross', whatever that means! For many people who do not believe that Jesus is the Son of God and for those who believe that He was only a prophet, this is where the story ends, but for the Christian it is just beginning.

Jesus died and was resurrected (brought back to life) again on the third day. After Christ went back to heaven, the disciples whom he taught while He was on Earth were now ready to start their work. In Christian terms we refer to this as their ministry— the office they were gifted to work in. The book of the Acts of the

Apostles (the fifth book of the New Testament) tells us how the disciples, now called the Apostles, continued the work that Jesus started. While Jesus was with them, teaching and training them, they followed Him; hence they were known as His disciples. However, when Jesus went up to heaven and was no longer with them, He commissioned them and 'sent them out' to preach the gospel far and wide and to set up the first churches. It was at this point that they became known as the Apostles (which means to be sent out or commissioned by someone).

"Jesus came up and said to them, 'All authority [all power of absolute rule] in heaven and on Earth has been given to Me. Go therefore and make disciples of all the nations [help the people to learn of Me, believe in Me, and obey My words], baptising them in the name of the Father and of the Son and of the Holy Spirit, teaching them to observe everything that I have commanded you; and lo, I am with you always [remaining with you perpetually—regardless of circumstance, and on every occasion], even to the end of the age.'"

[Matthew 28:18-20 AMP]

That commission has been given to all who come to the Lord, once we receive Him as our Lord and Saviour. It is our duty to tell others about Him so that they too may receive salvation. They in turn should spread the gospel from generation to generation until it reaches the ends of the Earth and everyone, at some time in their life, has been told about Jesus Christ. And this is what the Apostles did. Preaching and teaching the gospel, baptising the nations in the name of the Father, Son and Holy Spirit. This saw the emergence of Christianity and the first church came into being.

Recommended Reading

Matthew Chapters 1-2	The Birth of Jesus
John Chapter 2	The Beginning of Jesus' Ministry
John Chapter 15	Persecution and Rejection

ACTIVITY 3

How old was Jesus when His public ministry started? ....

What and where was His first miracle?..

....

Why did Jesus have to die? ....

....

....

What is the importance of not being distracted? ....

....

....

My life as a Christian will be stress-free. True or False?.....................

Discuss the above statement: ....

....

....

How many wise men came to Jesus' birth? ....

....

....

Notes: ....

....

....

....

....

....

....

Paid for in Blood

You paid the price that we might live
There's nothing more that You can give
For on that day when mankind fell
Our Father knew, He'd send Immanuel
To save the wretched world from sin
And the hopeless state that it was in.

In the garden, on the night You were betrayed
When on Your face, You fell and prayed
Your tears dropped heavy, like blood, on the ground
As You asked the Father if another way could be found
Yet from that cup You drank and took the bitter pill
We thank You for holding to our Father's will.

Upon the Cross You breathed Your last breath
But it was just the beginning, to conquer death
As the earth quaked and the rocks rent
Into the depths of hell You went
To take back what belonged to You
And to crush his head with Your shoe.

Your life you laid down to take it up again
As our Father sent down the Holy Rain
And when you awoke your bride was birthed
Just like Adam, after he came from the earth
With Your Blood You set us free...
And said... If I be lifted up I'll draw all men unto Me.

Still You intercede to our Father for Us
And fight our battles with Your name... Jesus!
Our love we send from our hearts to You
The One who is called 'Faithful and True'
We've been paid for by the Blood of the Lamb
And today we say Thank You to the Great I Am.

CHAPTER 4
THE FIRST CHURCH

Today the term 'church' is used interchangeably by many to mean both the building in which Christians worship and the people gathered together to worship. However, the true meaning of the term 'church' is not the building, but the people. The building in which Christians worship is the house of God. The first church was formed by the Apostles after Jesus ascended into heaven. They travelled through Jerusalem, Judea, Samaria, Antioch, Rome and throughout the world, preaching and teaching the gospel about Jesus and the kingdom of God. The church structure we are used to today did not exist.

Worship took place primarily in people's homes and anywhere else they were able to meet. Christians assembling together were known as the Church, and that is why the place in which they assembled also became known as the church. In the book of Acts, Saul, a Pharisee, hated the Church and the mention of Jesus' name so much that he started persecuting and killing Christians.

"But Saul began ravaging the church [and assaulting believers]; entering house after house and dragging off men and women, putting them in prison."

[Acts 8:3 AMP]

The above scripture confirms that there was no set place of worship and that it was the people who were called the Church. The Lord's Supper, or Holy Communion (the breaking of bread), was also organised from house to house as confirmed in Acts 2:46. The early church was spread all over Jerusalem and not restricted to one building. During these travels to Antioch, the Apostles assembled like-minded people and taught them. The true definition of the Church is the people who believe in Jesus Christ, and not the building. It is the heart of the believer that belongs to God, and the unshakeable love and faith in Him and Him alone that defines the Christian and the Church of God.

When Jesus returns for His Church, it is the people He will take with Him and not the buildings with their ornate stained-glass windows or accessories.

The term 'Christians' was first used in Antioch, and the people and place of worship became as one.
"And Barnabas left for Tarsus to search for Saul; and when he found him, he brought him back to Antioch. For an entire year they met [with others] in the church and instructed large numbers; and it was in Antioch that the disciples were first called Christians."

[Acts 11:25-26 AMP]

So, we know this was the start of Christianity and the first church, and that it has continued through the ages to today. Christianity has taken many turns and directions and had many ups and downs. Hundreds of denominations, along with inconsistent teachings and practices, have caused much confusion in the faith, and decades later the world is more confused now than ever. Prophecies are misunderstood and the deeper meanings of the Bible often misinterpreted, as scriptures are taken out of context. Some teachings are accepted while others are rejected. Man-made laws, traditions, practices and cultures, not to mention the cults and newly emerging religious groups, are mixed with Christian doctrine. Who can be blamed for being confused? A good rule of thumb here is to get to know the Bible for yourself, and have a real relationship with the Holy Spirit so He can guide you.

From the 1st century A.D. (Anno Domini, which means 'The Year of our Lord'), the Apostles started setting up the first churches. Christianity then went through the dark ages, when the gospel was so distorted that many innocent Christians died for no other reason than being true followers of Christ.

Christianity has since experienced many revivals, which is a refreshing of the faith where people's spiritual eyes are opened and they begin to search for God and give their lives to Jesus. During these revivals, we experience a real outpouring of the Holy Spirit. We see many miracles and there is a surge in the growth of the church.

The history of the Church and how it has evolved through the ages is a huge topic and only the briefest overview can be afforded at this point. It is recommended that you read the book of Acts to gain a better understanding of the Holy Spirit, the work of the Apostles and the emergence of the first church. The Church came into being during a time of violence and unrest. The Apostle Peter preached his first message and approximately three thousand people were saved that day.

"So then, those who accepted his message were baptised; and on that day about 3,000 souls were added [to the body of believers]. They were continually and faithfully devoting themselves to the instruction of the apostles, and to fellowship, to eating meals together and to prayers."

[Acts 2:41-42 AMP]

Many people who saw the miracles performed by the Apostles received the gospel and became Christians. The Apostles preached the true gospel of Jesus Christ without compromise, and the first Christians found comfort and support together during these troubled times. They sold all they owned and gave the money to Peter and the other Apostles to be shared out to everyone according to their individual needs. It is worth noting here that this was not a requirement of the faith; the first Christians received of God's love and freely gave all they had to build, strengthen and support the church.

It is these early beginnings that teach us that, as Christians, we should assemble to strengthen and support each other. But one question still remains; that is, how did we get from this church structure to the division, confusion and corruption in the various denominations today? As with all things, there is a beginning!

Corruption in the Church

Ananias and Sapphira were a husband and wife who joined the church after Peter's first message was preached. They chose of their own free will to sell their land and all their possessions and told Peter that they had given all the proceeds to the church. This, however, was a lie as they had kept some of the proceeds for themselves. The Holy Spirit revealed this deception to Peter, who confronted them, and then they fell to the ground and died. You may think this harsh, but Peter explains the depths of their deception:

"But Peter said, 'Ananias, why has Satan filled your heart to lie to the Holy Spirit and [secretly] keep back for yourself some of the proceeds [from the sale] of the land? As long as it remained [unsold], did it not remain your own [to do with as you pleased]? And after it was sold, was the money not under your control? Why is it that you have conceived this act [of hypocrisy and deceit] in your heart? You have not [simply] lied to people, but to God.'"

[Acts 5:3-4 AMP]

There was no need to lie; the land and the money belonged to them. They were lying to God and deceiving their fellow Christians by pretending to give more than they did, and this was the first entry of sin into the church, which God took very seriously. If the Holy Spirit had not revealed this to Peter they would have continued with their lies and manipulations, which would have wounded the first church greatly. The people were already suffering both at the hands of the Romans and thanks to the violent era in which the church was birthed.

Ananias and Sapphira allowed Satan to speak into their hearts, so when everyone else was exercising God's love, they were counteracting it with deceit. Remember, Satan constantly tries to counteract the good that God does. God knew this sin would grow and affect the church for generations to come, and it has. Today we have divisions in the church through lies and misappropriation of funds. God will always root out the cause and not nurse the symptoms of sin. Just as the first sin in mankind resulted in death, so too did the first sin in the church.

We see the actions of Ananias and Sapphira mirrored in many churches today, with people pretending to be what they are not, which always ends in hurt. This can and does happen with both leaders and members, and for these reasons it is so important to be in a close relationship with God so He can reveal these things to you just as He did to Peter. People can deceive other people, but they cannot deceive God!

Tithes and Offerings

Giving to the church is a constant 'bone of contention', with many Christians disputing whether they should give tithes [contributions] and offerings [monetary gifts] to the church or not. Should they give one tenth, should they give everything, should they give what they can or give nothing at all? In the Old Testament, Abraham gave tithes, and the Jewish people were instructed to give tithes to the priests who looked after the temple and prayed to God on their behalf. The definition of 'tithe' is one tenth of annual earnings, which was taken as a tax for the support of the church and the priests.

Through many generations people would pay one tenth of their earnings to the church, and this would be used for its upkeep, maintenance and paying the priests who were providing a service to the community, as this was their full-time job.

Many will say that one tenth of their earnings is too much, and all sorts of accusations are levelled at the church when people do not want to give anything to God. But money does not just appear; it must be given to the church for the working of the ministry. The New Testament does not force Old Testament laws onto the church today, but we should still have a willing heart to give to the work of the Lord. Church buildings have mortgages and rents to pay, loans, maintenance, tools and resources for services to the community. There is a cost for everything and, when exhausted, the storehouse needs to be replenished.

When the first church came into being, Jesus did not enforce any laws or instruct the Apostles as to what to do to raise funds for the church; neither did He rain down gold from heaven. If we dissect this argument a little further, those who think one tenth is too much to give will definitely not like the solution that evolved naturally when the first church came into being, which was for Christians to sell everything they had and give the proceeds to the church. Throughout the Bible, the Lord encourages us to give to the house of God, to give to the poor and to give to each other:

"Let each one give [thoughtfully and with purpose] just as he has decided in his heart, not grudgingly or under compulsion, for God loves a cheerful giver [and delights in the one whose heart is in his gift]. And God is able to make all grace [every favour and earthly blessing] come in abundance to you, so that you may always [under all circumstances, regardless of the need] have complete sufficiency in everything [being completely self-sufficient in Him], and have an abundance for every good work and act of charity [love]."

[2 Corinthians 9:7-8 AMP]

Here we are told to give from our hearts, not begrudgingly or because we want something in return, and that God loves the person who gives cheerfully. God is also saying that you will find favour in Him when you give, and He will provide for you the things you need in life. So, God is asking us to give what we decide, and from our hearts, but not to put a price on it and hold the Lord to ransom by deciding what we want in return.

"Looking up, He saw the rich people putting their gifts into the treasury. And He saw a poor widow putting in two small copper coins. He said, 'Truly I say to you, this poor widow has put in [proportionally] more than all of them; for they all put in gifts from their abundance; but she out of her poverty put in all she had to live on.'"

[Luke 21:1-4 AMP]

Because the widow gave everything, and from her heart, Jesus was pleased and, even though it was much less than what the others gave, it equated to more than all of them because it was ALL that she had. God is not telling us how much to give, but if we don't have great amounts, we should give what we can. To Him it is worth more than the lavish, elaborate amounts—not that there is anything wrong with those!

For those who reject the giving of the one tenth that was required in Old Testament times and claim we do not have to give to the church under the New Testament, there are consistent examples given in the New Testament where Christians give everything they have, which far exceeds one tenth of earnings. The first Christians, like the widow and her two mites, gave all they had. I can't imagine that there are many people these days who would give all that they own, and the Lord is not asking anyone to do this. His simple message is to give willingly, and from the heart, into God's treasury for the workings of the ministry. If you choose to give one tenth of your earnings then do so; if you decide on another amount then do that; if you choose to give what little you have or a lot, that's fine too, but do give to the work of God's church to spread the gospel across the world.

Recommended Reading

This would be a good time to start reading about the life of Jesus, His crucifixion and resurrection. You will gain a complete picture by reading the gospels in their entirety: Matthew, Mark, Luke and John in the New Testament.

ACTIVITY 4

Who formed the first church? ....

....

....

Who brought corruption into the church and what were the
consequences?...

....

....

How much in tithes and offerings should we give to the church? ....

....

....

Where was the term 'Christians' first used? ....

....

....

What does A.D. mean?..

....

Notes: ....

....

CHAPTER 5
THE THREE WORKS OF GRACE

"For it is by grace [God's remarkable compassion and favour drawing you to Christ] that you have been saved [actually delivered from judgment and given eternal life] through faith. And this [salvation] is not of yourselves [not through your own effort], but it is the [undeserved, gracious] gift of God; not as a result of [your] works [nor your attempts to keep the Law], so that no one will [be able to] boast or take credit in any way [for his salvation]."

Ephesians 2:8-9 AMP

Your journey in Christ will be the ultimate life experience, a new spiritual birth: speaking in a heavenly language (tongues), stepping into the supernatural (not voodoo, not witchcraft or anything sinister), living in the spirit and walking with God—life doesn't get any better. But being born again is not a physical rebirth or reincarnation. Nicodemus, a Jewish ruler, came to Jesus at night asking about the kingdom of heaven, and Jesus told him that no one can enter heaven without being born again, but He was talking about water baptism and a spiritual birth.

"Jesus answered him, 'I assure you and most solemnly say to you, unless a person is born again [reborn from above—spiritually transformed, renewed, sanctified], he cannot [ever] see and experience the kingdom of God.'"

[John 3:3 AMP]

Your rebirth is the start of your spiritual journey and you will be travelling with God from now on. He is your best friend and will be with you all the way; He will never leave you nor forsake you. This journey with God is a world that cannot be imagined but must be experienced. You will learn new ways of thinking, speaking, being and living by the power and strength of the Holy Spirit of God and not by your own strength. It will be the best journey ever!

Your early thought might be, 'I'm a Christian now—so what? Nothing has really changed for me. I still go to work, college, university or am still unemployed, so what's the big deal?' The big deal is that you have started on the greatest journey of your life. You just don't yet realise it!

Life doesn't slow down or stop for anyone, so you have to keep up with it, making sense of it as you go along. He will be with you when you are happy and when you are sad, when you are going through challenges and upheavals and when you think there is no way forward.

"God is our refuge and strength [mighty and impenetrable],
A very present and well-proved help in trouble.
Therefore we will not fear, though the earth should change
And though the mountains be shaken and slip into the heart of the seas."

[Psalm 46:1-2 AMP]

God is telling us that He is our protection and strength. He will help us in troubled times and we should not be fearful, regardless of how big our problems may seem. Sometimes you will feel His presence and other times you will think He has left you, but know that you are never alone. God always knows where you are and what you are going through.

The First Work of Grace - Salvation

The first leg of your journey is to receive the gift of salvation, which is to be 'saved' from sin. This is known as the first work of grace. Grace is showing favour and kindness to someone who has done nothing to deserve it; in fact, they have often done things against the person offering it.

God's grace is unparalleled and, even though we have done so many things against Him, He makes salvation available to everyone. When God breathed His eternal breath of life into making us, he made us spirit beings. The physical body is the only part of us that will die—our spirits will remain. Our bodies came from the earth and, when we die, our bodies will return to the earth. But the gift of salvation means that we are saved from eternal death.

God's ultimate gift to us, which we did nothing to deserve, and which we cannot buy regardless of how rich we are, is eternal life in love and peace and happiness with Him after our physical body dies.

This is 'salvation', which is often referred to as being 'saved'. This eternal reward is given freely when you say 'yes' to Jesus and make a choice to be a follower of Christ. The alternative is eternal life without Him in hell. Yes, as sure as there is a heaven, there is a hell, and it is not a nice place. Whichever path you choose, you will be living for all eternity, regardless of whether you accept the Lord or not, for your spirit will never die.

This book is not designed to judge or to use scare tactics, only to emphasise the truth to the new Christian, and anyone looking for answers in their life. Everything we do has consequences, whether we like it or not. The world is happy to accept the consequences dictated by 'man' but not the ones dictated by God. Hell was not created for us; it was created for Satan and his demons and evil spirits. Whatever the reason that causes you to leave this world without Christ in your life, the consequence is clear. Don't get angry and resentful; don't blame God or anyone else; just make the right choices and hold fast to them.

Getting this far on your journey wasn't easy, but you have already made the right choice, so let's look a little more closely at how you got here. What did you do to become a 'born-again Christian'? Why are you here and others aren't? Well, you got to this place in your life because you were 'called' by God into salvation and you answered the 'call', while others didn't. Before anyone can become a Christian, God has to 'draw' them to Him. This is also referred to as 'the call' of God. Jesus did this when He called the disciples, by saying to them 'Follow Me', and they did. It is a spiritual calling, initiated by God and delivered to us through His Holy Spirit, and not the other way around.

As stated earlier, Christians and non-Christians alike are baffled by God the Holy Spirit, but He is here and very real and you need to get to know Him. He speaks to our hearts and reveals the deeper things of Christ to us. All the things that God has prepared for us can only be revealed through His Holy Spirit.

"For God has unveiled them and revealed them to us through the [Holy] Spirit; for the Spirit searches all things [diligently], even [sounding and measuring] the [profound] depths of God [the divine counsels and things far beyond human understanding]. For what person knows the thoughts and motives of a man except the man's spirit within him? So also no one knows the thoughts of God except the Spirit of God. Now we have received, not the spirit of the world, but the [Holy] Spirit who is from God, so that we may know and understand the [wonderful] things freely given to us by God."

[1 Corinthians 2:10-12 AMP]

The spirit of a man knows only the man and does not know the things of God. Only the Spirit of God knows the things of God and reveals them to us. There is absolutely <u>no</u> other way that we can get to know God. No one can save you or offer you salvation, and you cannot pay for it. The Holy Spirit draws us to Christ, who saves us. We receive the gift of salvation the moment we accept Christ.

The Call to Salvation

People are called in different ways and everyone's testimony is unique to them. When Jesus declared to the Jews that God is His Father, they refused to believe Him. He continued to tell them that no one can be a believer in Him unless the Father draws them.

"No one can come to Me unless the Father who sent Me draws him [giving him the desire to come to Me]; and I will raise him up [from the dead] on the last day."

[John 6:44 AMP]

This is the way God has designed it and we cannot change it. We are drawn by hearing the preaching and teachings of the gospel, of Jesus Christ. When you have a sudden desire or a longing over a period of time to know more about God, to question your mortality, to walk away from the familiar to start seeking a greater purpose, a willingness to step into the unknown, this is the Holy Spirit drawing you.

When a Christian starts sharing their faith with you and invites you to church, or you are passing a church and have a desire to go in, this is the Lord drawing you to Him. Sometimes it is subtle and can happen over a period of time, and other times it is like an instant awakening in your spirit; however, it happens, and when it does happen, know that you are definitely being called by God.

Sometimes you know when and how it started, and other times you can't quite 'put your finger on it'; you just noticed there was a change in you. This world and all it has to offer was not satisfying you anymore.

God could have been calling you for many years, from childhood even, and you may have decided to answer that call many years later. The Lord will make Himself known to all of us at some time throughout our lives, but the important point to remember here is to be sure to 'answer that call'. Answering the 'call of God' is to accept the invitation to church, or to act on your desire to seek answers, questioning things and not being happy with the status quo. Ask God to reveal Himself to you. The Lord will work with the desires of your heart. If you decide to seek Him, you *will* find Him. Don't buy into the misconception that it doesn't matter how you live or how you die— it really does.

When we die as Christians, also referred to as 'dying in Christ', our spirit returns to be with God, but our bodies return to the earth. "Then the dust [out of which God made man's body] will return to the earth as it was, and the spirit will return to God who gave it."

[Ecclesiastes 12:7 AMP]

To be fully connected to the Lord and to receive salvation we need to accept Jesus as our Lord and Saviour, confess our sins to Him, ask for forgiveness and be repentant. The moment you make this declaration from your heart and mean it, you are saved. It is your heart that the Lord works with, so saying it with your lips and not meaning it in your heart is ineffective and of no use. Doing it to please someone or for your own hidden agenda will not be beneficial to you either because the Lord knows your heart. You will need to ask the Lord for forgiveness of all your sins, whether you were conscious of them or not, and promise never to go back to a sinful life.

Forgiveness

Forgiveness is the act or process of forgiving or pardoning someone. It is when you stop feeling anger towards the person and give up the right to seek justice or payment for whatever wrong was done to you. The Lord no longer feels anger towards us after the fall of mankind in the Garden of Eden because He has forgiven us. To repent is to be remorseful, to be sorry for the way you have lived, to turn away from sin and towards God with the intention of never going back to your old ways. It is saying sorry to the Lord, sincerely, from the heart.

An example could be: 'Lord, please forgive me for all the lies I have told, for the people I have hurt, for the many times I have deceived others. I promise never to return to that life again.' This is not to say that you will not slip, have moments of weakness and struggle sometimes. The Lord is merciful and He realises that you will make mistakes and struggle occasionally, so He will not punish you for it. When you do wrong and are genuinely sorry for it, you should confess it to the Lord and ask Him to forgive and strengthen you.

TAKE NOTE

Although Jesus died for our past, present and future sins, some Christians believe that we never have to ask the Lord for forgiveness, and that each time a Christian fails through weakness or temptation and feels deeply sorry for it, we only need to confess our wrongdoing and move on. This is incorrect teaching. To receive our Father's forgiveness, we must ask for it.

Confessing and repenting of sin includes asking for forgiveness. Indeed, Jesus teaches us how to pray to the Father by asking Him to forgive us as we also should forgive others, in the Lord's Prayer. And this is not a prayer to be prayed once. It is a prayer template on which prayers should be based.

"Pray, then, in this way:

'Our Father, who is in heaven,

Hallowed [blessed] be Your name.

Your kingdom come,

Your will be done

On Earth as it is in heaven.

Give us this day our daily bread.

And forgive us our debts, as we have forgiven our debtors [letting go of both the wrong and the resentment].

And do not lead us into temptation, but deliver us from evil. For Yours is the kingdom and the power and the glory forever. Amen.'"

[Matthew 6:9:13 AMP]

Jesus Himself taught us to pray in this way. If you are not sure what prayer is or how to pray, we will be covering this topic in Chapter 10. When you make a mistake and are truly remorseful in your heart, what is wrong with saying, 'Father, I have caused my friend pain (confession). I am truly sorry for this (repentance). Please forgive me (forgiveness); I won't do it again (repentance)'? It would take seconds to say that to our Father in heaven. How can that be wrong, and why would you do two thirds and leave out one from what is required to move on from the situation? Please let us not complicate our lives by choosing to obey some parts of the Bible and disregarding others. Life is capable of being complicated all by itself; no help is needed.

Just because the Lord will forgive us each time we ask doesn't mean that we should start sinning presumptuously and thinking 'it will be fine, I'll do it and ask the Lord to forgive me later and He will,' or 'all my sins are already forgiven so I'm alright'. This is setting a dangerous precedent. Remember, the Lord knows your heart and will turn away if you attempt to make a mockery of Him.

"Do not be deceived, God is not mocked [He will not allow Himself to be ridiculed, nor treated with contempt nor allow His precepts to be scornfully set aside]; for whatever a man sows, this and this only is what he will reap."

[Galatians 6:7 AMP]

The Lord will never condemn you if you are genuinely struggling with temptation and you have a real desire in your heart to stop doing whatever it is you continue to do. He will work in you to strengthen you. The conscious sins are easily identified:

"For the sinful nature has its desire which is opposed to the Spirit, and the [desire of the] Spirit opposes the sinful nature; for these [two, the sinful nature and the Spirit] are in direct opposition to each other [continually in conflict], so that you [as believers] do not [always] do whatever [good things] you want to do. But if you are guided and led by the Spirit, you are not subject to the

Law. Now the practices of the sinful nature are clearly evident: they are sexual immorality, impurity, sensuality [total irresponsibility, lack of self-control], idolatry, sorcery, hostility, strife, jealousy, fits of anger, disputes, dissensions, factions [that promote heresies], envy, drunkenness, riotous behaviour, and other things like these. I warn you beforehand, just as I did previously, that those who practice such things will not inherit the kingdom of God."

[Galatians 5:17-21 AMP]

When you are repentant and confess to the Lord, it is good practice and a requirement to really offload on Him. Tell Him everything; hold nothing back! Don't be afraid to say what you've done and speak honestly from the heart. This is the first step in your healing process. Hanging on to things and refusing to let go of them will only hinder your healing and prevent you from moving on. It is those things that will eventually come back and weaken you.

"Therefore humble yourselves under the mighty hand of God [set aside self-righteous pride], so that He may exalt you [to a place of honour in His service] at the appropriate time, casting all your cares [all your anxieties, all your worries, and all your concerns, once and for all] on Him, for He cares about you [with deepest affection, and watches over you very carefully]."

[1 Peter 5:6-7 AMP]

We must humble ourselves and tell the Lord about our problems. This is how God's grace works. Remember, we serve a God who doesn't sleep, is never tired of listening to us and is able to bring us through anything. He really can cope with billions of people casting their cares on Him all at once. Don't try to make sense of it, just do it! Get used to doing your part and letting God do His.

There are also forms of sin that we are not so conscious of and are not easily identified, so keep a check on these. Pride and vanity are right at the top of that list. They are difficult to identify in ourselves because we are misguided into believing we are humble when we are not. That we are doing something to help someone when in actual fact we are doing it to be rewarded for our actions. This can lead to boastfulness and not being able to take correction, or refusing to be guided in the right direction by those who are your leaders.

"Obey your [spiritual] leaders and submit to them [recognising their authority over you], for they are keeping watch over your souls and continually guarding your spiritual welfare as those who will give an account [of their stewardship of you]. Let them do this with joy and not with grief and groans, for this would be of no benefit to you."

[Hebrews 13:17 AMP]

Many unconscious sins derive from our personal beliefs on what we consider to be right or wrong. A common one is telling lies. Often, we justify a lie and say it was only a 'little white lie, no harm done'. A lie is a lie; it is neither white nor black and it is still sin. God doesn't like it.

No sin is too great for God to forgive. If you hear a little voice in your head telling you that you are too evil to be forgiven, that God couldn't possibly love you after all that you've done, reject those thoughts. Don't accept them into your psyche; they are damaging and will result in self-condemnation and guilt. Our God is able and willing to save and change anyone.

Accepting the Lord Jesus as your Lord and Saviour and repenting of your sins can be done all together in one simple prayer known as 'The Prayer of Salvation' or 'The Prayer of Acceptance'. If you've never prayed before, it will be your first prayer but definitely not your last.

The Prayer of Salvation

Dear Father in heaven, I come to you in the name of Jesus.
I am sorry for my sins and the way I have lived.
Forgive me, Lord, and cleanse me from all wrongdoings.
I confess that Jesus is my Lord and Saviour;
That He is the Son of God who died to set me free.
In my heart I believe God raised Jesus from the dead
And He is alive right now.
Jesus, please come into my life and save me!
I believe I'm alive, I'm born again and I'm saved.
Amen.

If you say this simple prayer, which can be varied to suit each person, from your heart, the Lord will hear you, and from that very moment you will be saved. God has forgiven you of ALL your sins and you have been accepted as a child of God. This is the start of the journey and not the end. When you come to the Lord, He wants you to be free; He will not condemn you for your past actions and does not want you to condemn yourself either. If you continue to feel condemned and guilty, what was the point of Him dying to set you free? Don't hold onto guilt!

"Therefore there is now no condemnation [no guilty verdict, no punishment] for those who are in Christ Jesus [who believe in Him as personal Lord and Saviour]. For the law of the Spirit of life [which is] in Christ Jesus [the law of our new being] has set you free from the law of sin and of death."

[Romans 8:1-2 AMP]

When you come to the Lord, your slate is wiped clean. Life is difficult enough without being constantly reminded of our failings and shortcomings, so He won't do that. This is instead a time for great rejoicing for the new convert and their friends and family. And if you have no friends or family to share this precious moment with you, make no mistake that God is overjoyed and there is great rejoicing in heaven, which is incomparable to our rejoicing.

"I tell you, in the same way there will be more joy in heaven over one sinner who repents than over ninety-nine righteous people who have no need of repentance."

[Luke 15:7 AMP]

So now you have made a commitment to God, what's next?

Public Declaration

Jesus led by example, so we follow His lead. He directed the Apostles to preach and teach and baptise people in the name of the Father, the Son and the Holy Spirit. The next step is the public declaration of your decision to answer God's call—water baptism. Jesus wasn't ashamed of us, or afraid to show His love for us and to call us His own, so we must not be ashamed of Him. If we deny Him, He will deny us, so although the water baptism doesn't save us, it is a very important part of our salvation.

"Therefore, the one who confesses and acknowledges Me before men [as Lord and Saviour, affirming a state of oneness with Me], that one I will also confess and acknowledge before My Father who is in heaven. But the one who denies and rejects Me before men, that one I will also deny and reject before My Father who is in heaven."

[Matthew 10:32-33 AMP]

Due to the stigma attached to religion in the world today and to the Christian faith, people often fear ridicule and persecution. Challenges from family and friends and the fear of how their news will be received often leaves new converts feeling confused, so they sometimes hide this singularly most important decision of their lives from anyone who may disapprove. We must be steadfast in our convictions and not be intimidated or be ashamed of the Lord. Denying Him is not a nice thing to do and you wouldn't do that to someone you love.

Water baptism is to be fully immersed into water and to surface again. This represents the burial of the 'old sinful person' and the birth of the 'new person' in Christ. Hence the term 'born-again Christian'. Just as Christ was buried and resurrected, the water baptism represents our burial and resurrection in Him. Thank the Lord that we don't actually have to go through what He went through! We do not have to be crucified and to suffer as Jesus did, so let us not be afraid to do this simple act for the Lord.

TAKE NOTE

If someone is on their deathbed, whether young or old, and they accept the Lord there and then, God will forgive them. The fact that they are too ill to be baptised in water does not mean that they are not saved and, if they die shortly afterward, as long as their heart completely accepted Jesus as their Lord and Saviour, then they are with the Lord.

I'm not saying that you should wait until you are dying to accept the Lord in order to bypass living the life of a Christian or making a public declaration. If you plan to wait until you are old or dying to try to trick your way out of living a righteous life, remember the

Holy Spirit will know this. Plus, no one knows exactly when or how they will die. How many people get any kind of warning before their death? Don't play games!

The Second Work of Grace - Sanctification

Your journey continues with the cleaning-up process, the second work of grace, known as Sanctification. Again, this is referred to as a work of grace because the Lord is not under any obligation to do it. He does it because of His love for us and because, if we are to get into a close relationship with Him—as He is holy, and we are not—we must be cleaned up so that He can work with us. This is the cleansing of the person we used to be and is a process that continues throughout the life of a Christian.

Many Christians think that once they accept Jesus as their Lord and Saviour, this is where the journey ends, and they don't allow the Lord to clean them up. They continue life just as they did before: swearing, clubbing, getting drunk and such-like, but now they go to church as well. This is not sanctification! You are preventing the Holy Spirit from performing the second work of grace in you when you continue to live as you did before.

When we are in the world our minds are blind to the truth of Jesus Christ and our spiritual eyes are not yet open. We think there is no God, so we live the way we want to. We were born in sin, so we are corrupted by it. The Holy Spirit must now change our way of thinking, so the battle is in our minds—the way we think, our reasoning and our understanding. We are all controlled by our minds, and it is this part of us that poses the greatest challenge to our acceptance of the truth. The gospel is veiled or hidden from us when we are lost in sin, because we are blinded by Satan.

"But even if our gospel is [in some sense] hidden [behind a veil], it is hidden [only] to those who are perishing; among them the god of this world [Satan] has blinded the minds of the unbelieving to prevent them from seeing the illuminating light of the gospel of the glory of Christ, who is the image of God."

[2 Corinthians 4:3-4 AMP]

We all know how difficult it is to change someone's mind once it has been made up, and how difficult it is for someone to change our mind once we have decided on something. How many years did it take you to believe that Jesus Christ is the Son of God and died for you? My point exactly! When we come to the Lord, the Holy Spirit starts to change the way we think. He reminds us of who we are when our behaviour is inappropriate; this is known as convicting us.

He works with our spirit to reveal truths about Jesus Christ and the kingdom of heaven. Often you don't realise how much you have changed until you are faced with certain challenges where the 'old you' would have reacted in a certain way (got angry, sworn or lied) but you surprise yourself by acting calmly, reasoning with someone and admitting the truth. Suddenly you think, 'What just happened? That's not me. Why didn't I get angry?' Then the penny drops! 'I've changed—wow, how did I get to this place?' That is the work of the Holy Spirit; don't forget to thank Him.

It is a process by which your mind becomes more open to the possibilities, realities and truth of the spiritual world. Our mind is strong while at the same time fragile. Things can happen in our lives that impact our minds and the way we think, including the way we see ourselves and others. When we are happy, we feel good, empowered and enjoy life, but when we are sad, we can become depressed, see no point to living and can do the unthinkable. That is how powerful the mind is: it can tell you there is no point to life, and you act on it.

Satan knows this, so he attempts to control our minds by blinding us to the truth, creating a hold over us that is difficult to break. The Holy Spirit will not possess us or take control of our minds; He will not force anything on us, so if we don't want Him to work with us, He won't. When the Lord calls us, He waits for us to answer.
"Behold, I stand at the door and knock. If anyone hears My voice and opens the door, I will come in to him and dine with him, and he with Me."

[Revelation 3:20 NKJV]

The Devil has no such qualms. He is forceful and uses trickery, deceit, manipulation and lies to get what he wants. Many people have heard the saying, 'the truth will set you free', but may not know that it is actually a verse from the Bible or what it really means.
"And you shall know the truth, and the truth shall make you free."

[John 8:32 NKJV]

When we answer His call, the Holy Spirit starts cleaning up our minds and the way we think to reveal the truth of Jesus Christ to us. And it is the knowledge of that truth that sets us free from the hold that Satan has on us. During the sanctification process you will not be a bystander. You will play a part in it—a very important part—but you must have a desire to change from the old you. Check yourself, think before you speak and act, and be more aware of your thoughts than before.

"Regarding your previous way of life, you put off your old self [completely discard your former nature], which is being corrupted through deceitful desires, and be continually renewed in the spirit of your mind [having a fresh, untarnished mental and spiritual attitude], and put on the new self [the regenerated and renewed nature], created in God's image [godlike], in the righteousness and holiness of the truth [living in a way that expresses to God your gratitude for your salvation]."

[Ephesians 4:22-24 AMP]

Note here that 'you put off', not the Holy Spirit, and 'you put on', not the Holy Spirit. You must play your part, but the Holy Spirit will assist you in the process.

The Third Work of Grace - Baptism of the Holy Spirit

You have been called by God and you have answered the call, declaring the Lord Jesus as your Lord and Saviour with a public declaration of water baptism and sanctification. Now you *need* to be empowered for the journey ahead by the third work of grace, the Baptism of the Holy Spirit. From the beginning of mankind and throughout the Old Testament, God the Father is the person of the Godhead who spoke the world into being. He led the Hebrews out of Egypt and away from a cruel set of people by leading them through the wilderness to safety. He appeared in a cloud by day and fire by night to guide and protect them.

"The [presence of the] Lord was going before them by day in a pillar [column] of cloud to lead them along the way, and in a pillar of fire by night to give them light, so that they could travel by day and by night."

[Exodus 13:21 AMP]

Though Jesus and the Holy Spirit were also active at that time, it was not their time to be at the forefront rescuing man from his plight. Two thousand years ago was Jesus' time, when He was born in the flesh to save mankind. He lived among us, spreading the gospel and ushering in the birth of the Church and a new era. In fact, His appearance on the Earth was so great that He divided the eras. B.C. stands for 'Before Christ', and A.D. (Anno Domini) means 'The Year of our Lord' and is used when referring to the time after Christ.

A quick word about the eras. Many who refuse to accept Jesus also refuse to use A.D. and instead will use C.E., which means 'Common Era', and B.C.E., 'Before Common Era'. As a Christian, this is disrespectful to the Lord. Know that the coming of Christ is the single most important event that took place, which caused the eras to be divided. The world witnessed the undeniable power of our Lord of Glory, through whom all things were created, yet continues to deny Him.

Now is the time of the Holy Spirit. When Jesus went back up to heaven, He promised to send us the Comforter, who would help us, teach and guide us and give us peace during times of trouble and turmoil. The Holy Spirit reveals our purpose to us and empowers us for the journey ahead to fulfil our destiny in Christ. Jesus speaks of Him many times in the gospels.

"But the Helper [Comforter, Advocate, Intercessor, Counsellor, Strengthener, Standby], the Holy Spirit, whom the Father will send in My name [in My place, to represent Me and act on My behalf], He will teach you all things."

[John 14:26 AMP]

The Holy Spirit now dwells with us on the Earth. He is the active person of the Godhead, at the forefront, leading us into all truths. When you become a Christian, you should seek to be immersed, to be filled to overflowing with the power of the Holy Spirit.

"But you will receive power and ability when the Holy Spirit comes upon you."

[Acts 1:8 NKJV]

You do this through spending time in prayer and immersing yourself in the study of the Bible, as well as having a deep desire for the things of God and asking Him to baptise you in His Holy Spirit.

The baptism of the Holy Spirit is the most amazing experience and each person's is different. You will feel an overwhelming power emanating from your inner being as the Holy Spirit joins with your spirit to become one. But the power is always coming from the Holy Spirit and not from ourselves.

There is a lot of misconception about being filled with the Holy Spirit and the Baptism of the Holy Spirit. Being filled with the Holy Spirit is implicit when we accept Christ as our Lord and Saviour and are baptised and reborn into Christ. The Holy Spirit dwells within us at the point of salvation. Father, Son and Holy Spirit dwell within us as ONE. We are called by The Holy Spirit and He baptises us into the Body of Christ. This cannot happen without Him.

"For by one [Holy] Spirit we were all baptised into one body [spiritually transformed—united together], whether Jews or Greeks [Gentiles], slaves or free, and we were all made to drink of one [Holy] Spirit [since the same Holy Spirit fills each life]."

[1 Corinthians 12:13 AMP]

This is different from the Baptism of the Holy Spirit, although both terms are used interchangeably. The Baptism of the Holy Spirit is another DIMENSION of power to empower us for ministry and throughout our Christian journey, imparting the gifts of the Spirit to us by anointing us.

Tongues

The first evidence of the Baptism of the Holy Spirit is speaking in tongues—other languages or dialects—but there are other evidences also. You won't understand what you are saying but your intellect will be trying to work it out. This is futile; it is born of the Spirit and operates in your spirit, not your mind. However, through the process of time and spiritual maturity you can begin to receive understanding and insight.

"And they were all filled [that is, diffused throughout their being] with the Holy Spirit and began to speak in other tongues [different languages], as the Spirit was giving them the ability to speak out [clearly and appropriately]."

[Acts 2:4 AMP]

The Holy Spirit will give you the utterance and you respond by opening yourself, embracing the gift and not resisting. You will feel the overflow rising inside you and you should not attempt to constrain it. As you receive the utterance, you speak by faith, not worrying about the fact that you don't understand what you are saying.

Some Christians have never received the Baptism of the Holy Spirit with the evidence of speaking in tongues, and I have no answer for this, except you will need to spend time with the Lord and seek Him with all your heart. Ask Him why you haven't yet been filled; He will answer you and guide you. It may be a lack of understanding or it may be a lack of belief in the Holy Spirit, but He is the only one who can clarify this for you.

Speaking in tongues is not something we can conjure up; it is a gift that we have access to and all of us can and should receive the Baptism of the Holy Spirit. Please do not think that if you have never spoken in tongues you will not go to heaven. This is not a pre-requisite for heaven, it is a gift from God. There are many other spiritual gifts that the Lord blesses us with, all from the same Spirit and dependent on what we have been called into the kingdom to do. Only He can bestow spiritual gifts on you, which will empower you to fulfil your purpose.

"Now there are [distinctive] varieties of spiritual gifts [special abilities given by the grace and extraordinary power of the Holy Spirit operating in believers], but it is the same Spirit [who grants them and empowers believers]. And there are [distinctive] varieties of ministries and service, but it is the same Lord [who is served]. And there are [distinctive] ways of working [to accomplish things], but it is the same Go d who produces all things in all believers [inspiring, energising, and empowering them]."

[1 Corinthians 12:4-6 AMP]

When you come to the Lord, He will not throw all these gifts at you, because you would not be able to cope with them, and you were not called to be all things to all people. You would not appreciate them, would not know how to use them and, more importantly, you would never know the true value of them. As you become spiritually mature you can use your gifts more effectively, so the Lord will bless you according to your purpose. If you are called into the kingdom to heal the sick, He will bless you with gifts of healing, miracles and great faith.

But remember, the greater the calling, the greater the persecutions both from your own people and others—the ones you trust the most may let you down. People will be envious and jealous simply because God has placed a great calling on your life. During these times, always remember that Jesus did nothing wrong and He was hated, lied about and persecuted. I'm not saying you will be crucified, but you will go through many ordeals.

Remember that you were not called by 'man', so do not let anyone cause you to walk away from the Lord and lose your salvation. On the day of judgement, you cannot say you did this or that because of your brother or your sister or your spouse; you have to answer for your own actions. Your journey is between you and God and, although you will meet and befriend many people on the Christian journey, they cannot think for you, act for you or go through your experiences for you; it has to be between you and God.

Some Christians can be filled with the Baptism of the Holy Spirit and speak in tongues for the first time once they have accepted Jesus and before they have been water-baptised, some shortly after water baptism, some years later and some never.

A golden rule to remember is not to concern yourself with how long it took someone else to be filled with the Baptism of the Holy Spirit and do not measure yourself against anyone. It will just make you anxious and your focus will shift from spending time with the Lord to worrying about what someone else is doing. Just seek God and keep seeking Him on the matter.

"Ask, and it will be given to you; seek, and you will find; knock, and it will be opened to you. For everyone who asks receives, and he who seeks finds, and to him who knocks it will be opened."

[Matthew 7:7-8 NKJV]

In His Presence

When the Holy Spirit begins to work with your spirit, to fill you to overflowing and bless you with gifts, you will find that there are times when you cannot stand in His presence as His power is so great. Our bodies and spirit are not used to this pure, holy power now residing and working in us. You will experience many things that your mind will try to comprehend. There are many scriptures in the Bible that tell us when the power of God came upon someone they could not stand; they lost all the strength in their bodies. We often refer to this as 'falling out in the spirit'. This is not something to fear, but a good thing. We are not 'slain' or hurt; actually we are more refreshed and alive following the experience.

Many people, even some Christians, will say we should never fall out when the power of the Holy Spirit comes upon us. I would say that those people have not experienced the power of the Holy Spirit in their lives. The great prophet Daniel lost the strength in his body and fell to the ground when he was in the presence of an angel:

"So I was left alone and saw this great vision; yet no strength was left in me, for my normal appearance turned to a deathly pale, and I grew weak and faint [with fright]. Then I heard the sound of his words; and when I heard the sound of his words, I fell on my face in a deep sleep, with my face toward the ground."

[Daniel 10:8-9 AMP]

The scripture above is very clear. Daniel was in a 'deep sleep on his face'. People will try to use their intellect and limited understanding of God to explain what they themselves don't understand or what scares them. The men who were with Daniel ran off because they were scared, and this is true in life. People will run away from the scary or uncomfortable subjects.

Don't start doubting your relationship with God and the experiences you've had through Him because someone else who doesn't know Him is trying to tell you about your experiences. Don't assign these amazing workings to something or someone else and end up not giving God the praise for the things He is doing in your life. We do not work ourselves into a frenzy, then pass out, as many believe; we must know who we are in Christ and defend our faith without apologising for it. A good response to such a challenge could be, 'If you don't know my God, please don't try to tell me who you think He is, because I know Him. Get to know Him yourself and then we can talk.'

When the Holy Spirit first started working with me, I couldn't stop shaking. I was on the floor the moment I felt His presence, so naturally I inherited the nickname 'Shaky'. I felt His amazing power from the core of my being and all my strength left me as I slipped to the ground again and again, supported by my fellow Christians. As you become more used to the Holy Spirit dwelling in you and working with you, you will not always lose the strength in your body, but it does depend on how much of His power He bestows on you at that time and throughout your journey. The experience is like no other and the peace you will feel in your spirit is incomparable.

Recommended Reading

Ephesians Chapter 2	God's Grace
Romans Chapter 10	Salvation
1 Thessalonians Chapter 4	Sanctification

ACTIVITY 5

List the three works of grace:..

....

....

Why is it important to publicly declare your love for Jesus? ....

....

....

Which truth sets us free? ....

....

....

Which person of the Godhead is currently on Earth with us? ....

....

....

Name one evidence that you have received the Baptism of the Holy
Spirit. ....

....

Notes: ....

....

....

....

....

....

....

....

CHAPTER 6
FINDING YOUR PURPOSE

God has called you for a purpose and you must seek with all your heart to find out what that purpose is. Many new Christians find it difficult to know when the Holy Spirit is speaking to them. This is also true of some Christians who have been with the Lord for quite some time. The reason for this is because your spirit is not yet trained to hear His voice.

The way to train your spirit to hear the voice of the Holy Spirit is first to have an insatiable appetite for the Word of God—studying the Bible, knowing it and living it, allowing it to saturate your spirit. Remember, new babes in Christ need to be fed with 'milk', which is the Word of God. Secondly, you will need to spend much time in prayer to condition your spirit to be able to receive inspiration, visions, knowledge and the purpose for your life from God. It is a must that you spend real quality time with God to find out what His perfect will is for you. You have a great God, who creates greatness, so don't settle for being average by refusing to spend time with Him. He did not call you to be average; you were average before He called you. He called you for greatness!

Find out why you were born, why you have been called into the kingdom, what His purpose for the rest of your life is; don't guess, know! The Holy Spirit will anoint you for the work ahead. When the Holy Spirit 'anoints' you to work in the kingdom, He will set you apart, give you the authority and equip you with the gifts required to fulfil your purpose. In setting you apart, He will empower you with gifts that will begin to manifest and become apparent in you. For example, if you are called to prophesy, God will tell you what He wants you to say to the church, confirm when you should say it and guide you as to how to deliver His message. When He starts doing this in someone's life, He is setting them apart, anointing them to fulfil this purpose. Not everyone will be able to prophesy, only those anointed to do so.

Life without purpose is no life at all. It is often said that we live, we die and there is nothing after death. If that was correct, then there really wouldn't be any point to life, but that is very far from the truth. We are not just physical beings, we are predominantly spirit beings and we have a soul.

"And may your spirit and soul and body be kept complete and [be found] blameless at the coming of our Lord Jesus Christ."

[1 Thessalonians 5:23 AMP]

Put simply, man is a spirit who has a soul, and both the spirit and soul dwell in a physical body.

THE HUMAN SPIRIT

Dwells within the person and is the heart of the person. It consists of our sub-conscious and intuition.

This is our 'spirit man' and it is in our spirit that the Holy Spirit resides. Our spirit is eternal.

When we desire to follow the Lord in our hearts, the challenge takes place in our mind and our intellect.

The Holy Spirit works with our spirit to reveal the things of God. He identifies with our spirit as it was God who breathed His breath of life into us to give us the human spirit.

The more we live in the spirit, the more He can feed the intuitive part of us.

THE SOUL

Consists of our mind, intellect, will and emotions. Our soul is eternal also. It is our thought and reasoning function without the control of the Holy Spirit; that is why it is often referred to as fleshy and sinful.

In the soulish realm, if someone hurts you, accidentally or otherwise, your emotions are wounded.

The challenge is: do you resort to the spirit man to forgive, love and show mercy, allowing the Holy Spirit to heal your wounds, or do you resort to the flesh man and seek vengeance?

Our logic is what keeps us from hearing the voice of the Holy Spirit as we keep trying to find a logical explanation.

THE BODY

Is the physical house of the spirit and the soul, the container that carries everything. This is the 'flesh man' and it is this part of us that dies when we experience death.

The soul and the spirit do not die.

Both soul and spirit have expression through the physical body.

The flesh will use intellect and its own reasoning to reject the will of the spirit. We are born in sin with a corruptible body, so it is in our nature to challenge righteous-ness. It is this nature and the will of the flesh that must be brought under subjection to the spirit. We will be faced with this struggle throughout our Christian life.

So, man, a tri-partite being, exists in three parts that make up the whole. To function effectively in this physical life all three parts must work as one in purpose and will. The moment one part of our being is out of balance, things start going wrong. Many people accept the physical body and the soul but struggle to understand the eternal spirit within us. For this reason, many believe that when we die there is no more consciousness, the body is gone, the pain stops and we are buried six feet under or cremated, so that's the end of that. That could not be further from the truth! What about the spirit? Are we really to believe that such a complex being lives for no reason at all and all the joys and pains of life just die and disappear into nothingness?

When we die, the spirit passes on to a different reality outside of the physical realm. There are so many testimonies of people dying or who have died and come back to tell us of their experiences, so we really need to take heed. What would be the point of creating such a beautiful world? The fact that man has destroyed so much of it doesn't make it any less beautiful. Just take a moment to look up into the sky and meditate on it. The sun, the moon, the stars! There must be something greater than us out there that we will never truly understand.

Whenever we don't understand something, we tend to reject it or try to destroy it. Because we do not fully understand God, we reject him. Yet so many people are happy to believe in strange and destructive supernatural phenomena, to believe in men no greater than themselves and to depend on their own logic even though it is flawed, and they continue to fail.

We need purpose in our lives because, without a purpose, many find it difficult to wake up in the morning or to function as they should. Many find it difficult to deal with disappointments, grief, life's challenges and, even when they experience moments of happiness, they cannot fully enjoy them. For many of us who have experienced a loved one committing suicide, when you dig deep into the reasons and try to make sense of it, one thing will keep surfacing and that is their feeling of having no purpose in their lives.

I'm not speaking of living for a husband or wife or kids or a new job, I am talking about that deep, fulfilling purpose that gives life to someone's spirit. The 'Why am I here?' question, which can and often does have catastrophic consequences if there is no answer. Because of the misconception that when we die there is no more pain and no more consciousness, many commit suicide to stop that pain—to rest in peace. But this is not the case and, as Christians, we need to help people to understand this.

The Christian has hope in Jesus Christ and belief in eternal peace; the Christian has a purpose in life. Those living without hope or purpose often see no point to life. It holds no value for them; they can take their life and others' in a heartbeat and never feel remorse. People need to hear the message of Christ to give them hope.
"And He said to them, 'Go into all the world and preach the gospel to all creation. He who has believed [in Me] and has been baptised will be saved [from the penalty of God's wrath and judgment]; but he who has not believed will be condemned.'"

[Mark 16:15-16 AMP]

All Christians have a general purpose to spread the gospel, but we also have a more specific and individual purpose in life, and it is this that we need to seek from the Lord. When seeking your purpose, you will need advice and support from godly people, leaders and fellow Christians who have been through this process themselves.

You will need to identify the people preaching good, sound doctrine and learn from them. Although you will receive support from mature Christians, your purpose can only be revealed to you by God. Do not try to make it happen through your own efforts and don't be envious of what someone else is doing. God has more than enough for everyone. Don't restrict your spiritual growth by insisting that you are called to be one thing when the Lord is trying to tell you that He has called you for something else.

This can happen when you see a Christian prophesying because they have been given this gift by God to fulfil their purpose of bringing God's word to His people. You can admire this gift and even have a desire for it, but if you decide you would like this gift so much so that you become envious, pray for it and only it, and tell yourself that this is what you are called to do, you can hinder your progress. You are preventing the Lord from working with you because He cannot get through to you to tell you that you have been called to do something else.

Eventually you could be so driven by your personal desires that you decide to use your own abilities to start bringing messages to the church. Of course, the enemy will be right in the thick of it. If it is not of God, it will not grow or flourish and you will have wasted valuable time trying to be what you are not. Don't try to tell God what He created you for, let Him tell you what you were created for. You may want to walk in the prophetic ministry, but what if you are called to be a preacher or teacher of the gospel? What if you are called to be an evangelist? Is this calling any less worthy than that of prophecy? God knows our capabilities better than we do because He designed us for a specific purpose. We need to be open to the possibilities and trust God to guide us. Remember this is a journey of faith, towards trusting completely in Him.

Often as Christians we get impatient and want things to happen *now*, and if they don't, we give up. But God's time is not our time; there is no timeframe on when you will receive the Baptism of the Holy Spirit or when your purpose will be revealed to you or when you will receive all that God has for you. While salvation is instant, sanctification is ongoing throughout your life and purpose is also lifelong if you allow the Holy Spirit to work with you. Your purpose should be God's purpose for your life!

"Now may the God of peace Himself sanctify you through and through [that is, separate you from profane and vulgar things,

make you pure and whole and undamaged—consecrated to Him—
set apart for His purpose]."

[1 Thessalonians 5:23 AMP]

Be A Game-Changer

For so long your world was upside down but now it is turned the
right way up. Make no mistake, Satan does not like this; he is angry
(actually, he always is). Let us remind ourselves of what we are
dealing with here. Satan challenges God at every turn. He knows
there is no forgiveness for him, so he hates the fact that there is
forgiveness for us. He seeks to destroy Christians at every turn.
"The thief [Satan] does not come except to steal, and to kill, and to
destroy."

[John 10:10 NKJV]

This is Satan's purpose, to steal your salvation, to kill you and to
destroy your life, and not just yours, but your family's and friends'
all at the same time. He will use you to harm others and then destroy
you afterwards, if you let him. It is all a game to him, so when he
brings his game to you, you need to be a game-changer. You need
strategy, spiritual weapons and endurance. There is only one way
you can be victorious over him and that is through Jesus Christ.
There is power in the name of Jesus and everything you do must be
in His name. God gave Him this name because of the power in it.
"For this reason also [because He obeyed and so completely
humbled Himself], God has highly exalted Him [Jesus] and
bestowed on Him the name which is above every name, so that at
the name of Jesus every knee shall bow [in submission], of those
who are in heaven and on earth and under the earth, and that every
tongue will confess and openly acknowledge that Jesus Christ is
Lord [sovereign God], to the glory of God the Father."

[Philippians 2:9-11 AMP]

Satan and all his demons must bow to the name of Jesus. Whilst
we acknowledge what Satan is capable of, we do not fear him. All
he had to do in heaven was look beautiful, worship God and be a
leader over the angels under him, and he couldn't even do that! He
could not fulfil his purpose and he does not want you to fulfil yours,
so do not fear a continual failure. He does not know what you are

thinking unless you vocalise it. He cannot take your life because he did not create you and God will not allow it (however, he can convince you to do it or convince some else to do it, and he uses underhand methods and tactics).

He cannot create because he is a created being. In a word, he is limited in what he can do to you. His strategy is to remind you of your past sins, keep throwing the same temptations back at you and sometimes throw you some curve balls when you least expect it. So you need to know the game. The only way you will know the game is through revelations from the Holy Spirit, and to gain those, you need to have a relationship with Him.

When someone hurts you, Satan will convince your mind to seek revenge and to hurt them back. Our natural logic will want us to get even. He will use unwitting friends, family and acquaintances to convince you that what you are doing is right. This is his game plan, but don't play it with him—change the game. Do it God's way and love those who hurt you; the enemy will hate it, but there is nothing he can do because you have the power of the Holy Spirit protecting you and he cannot take on the Holy Spirit. He cannot win. But this is not to say he won't keep trying. Take advice and counsel from wise men and women of God and, more importantly, be led by the Holy Spirit. You can turn Satan's games on him, and this is how you do it:

"You have heard that it was said, 'An eye for an eye, and a tooth for a tooth [punishment that fits the offense].' But I say to you, do not resist an evil person [who insults you or violates your rights]; but whoever slaps you on the right cheek, turn the other toward him also [simply ignore insignificant insults or trivial losses and do not bother to retaliate—maintain your dignity, your self-respect, your poise]. If anyone wants to sue you and take your shirt, let him have your coat also [for the Lord repays the offender]. And whoever forces you to go one mile, go with him two. Give to him who asks of you, and do not turn away from him who wants to borrow from you.

"You have heard that it was said, 'You shall love your neighbour [fellow man] and hate your enemy.' But I say to you, love [that is, unselfishly seek the best or higher good for] your enemies and pray for those who persecute you, so that you may [show yourselves to] be the children of your Father who is in heaven; for He makes His sun rise on those who are evil and on those who are good, and makes the rain fall on the righteous [those who are morally upright] and the unrighteous [the unrepentant, those who oppose Him]. For if you love [only] those who love you, what reward do you have? Do not even the tax collectors do that? And if you greet only your brothers [wishing them God's blessing and peace], what more [than others] are you doing? Do not even the Gentiles [who do not know the Lord] do that? You, therefore, will be perfect [growing into spiritual maturity both in mind and character, actively integrating godly values into your daily life], as your heavenly Father is perfect."

[Matthew 5:38-48 AMP]

In the days of Jesus, the tax collectors were ruthless businessmen, squeezing taxes out of the poor, and were greatly disliked by the community and not held in high esteem. Jesus is saying here that even the cruel tax collectors with low morals who cared for no one could do the easy things such as be kind to those who were kind to them. God will not reward you for doing this. This is no challenge to Satan's plans for the child of God—don't play with him.

When you love those who hate you, it weakens Satan's hold on you. His strategy cannot stand against God's strategy. Throughout your journey you must strive to be like God. God's ways are not our ways, but we should try to be more like Him. The fruit of the Holy Spirit describes the characteristics and attributes of God that we should aspire to.

"But the fruit of the Spirit [the result of His presence within us] is love [unselfish concern for others], joy, [inner] peace, patience [not the ability to wait, but how we act while waiting], kindness, goodness, faithfulness, gentleness, self-control. Against such things there is no law."

[Galatians 5:22-23 AMP]

One fruit, nine attributes. You are a game-changer when the fruit of the Holy Spirit becomes first nature to you. These are the characteristics of God, and He has equipped us with everything we need in order to have a godly character. It is not an impossibility. The Bible does not say that we can attain sinless perfection, but we can keep striving to be perfect in Christ and we can sin less.

FRUIT OF THE SPIRIT

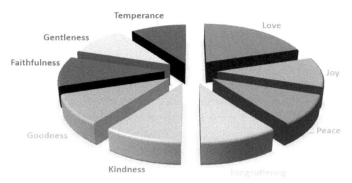

The Fruit of the Spirit

Learning to be like God is everything to a Christian. If we continue to think and behave as we did before we became Christians, while we were still in the world, then we give the enemy a way into our lives and a continuous hold over us. If he knows our weakness is anger and revenge and we do not allow the Holy Spirit to work in this area of our lives, we will fail each time we are challenged or tested.

You know you're a game-changer when you love unconditionally, have joy in the midst of pain, peace when wars are raging, suffer long when nothing is changing, show gentleness when met with aggression, exchange goodness for evil deeds, walk by faith in the wilderness, repay evil with kindness and exert self-control in the ultimate test!

God's Will

Without great trust in and reliance on God, you cannot change the game on the enemy or find your purpose. Your Christian journey is one of faith, and faith is a COMPLETE trust in God to bring you through.

Let us take a deeper look at what trusting in God really means for the Christian. We are living in a fallen world, and we have a real adversary snapping at our heels. Many things will happen to us, even though we are Christians. There will be good times and amazing times and then there will be bad times. We will die like everyone else, we may experience sickness, we will suffer both for our faith and otherwise at the hands of people who are dear to us as well as strangers. We cannot pretend that, when we come to the Lord, everything in this world will be perfect for us. The Lord does not promise this.

The greatest test for a Christian is how we behave when we go through ordeals and when we are suffering because things are not going the way we planned. When things are going well, we are happy and we have a good measure of faith, but when things are not going so well, our faith can be weakened. The true doctrine of faith in Jesus Christ is sometimes distorted with many variations in people having faith in themselves, or teachings that 'if you believe it then it is so'. No! This is not so. You can believe it all you want, but if it is not in Jesus Christ and the power and might of the Holy Spirit, then it will not be so.

People often put their trust in 'fate', 'luck' and 'chance', saying that if it happens, it happens, which has nothing to do with real destiny and purpose. We fight to try to get what we want in our own way, but we do not ask God for it, and, when we do eventually ask, we ask the wrong way by making it about ourselves and what is pleasing to us and not to God.

"You are jealous and covet [what others have] and your lust goes unfulfilled; so you murder. You are envious and cannot obtain [the object of your envy]; so you fight and battle. You do not have because you do not ask [it of God]. You ask [God for something] and do not receive it, because you ask with wrong motives [out of selfishness or with an unrighteous agenda], so that [when you get what you want] you may spend it on your [hedonistic] desires."

[James 4:2-3 AMP]

We long for things we don't have, even kill for them, and still cannot get them. We expect to get what we want immediately, to receive what we ask for on our terms, and when we don't get it, we lose faith. We blame God because we cannot understand why we didn't get what we wanted and we certainly don't want to accept no for an answer.

First, we always want the answer to be 'yes' and this will not always be the case. If it was, we would become spoilt and ungrateful.

Second, we often ask for what we want and ignore what we really need, but God sees our needs as well as our desires. We do not have the full picture, but He does, and He will give to us accordingly. Third, we are here to do God's will and not the other way around.

When Jesus prayed in the Garden of Gethsemane, He already knew exactly what would happen to Him. He was deeply troubled and the Bible tells us that His soul was exceedingly sorrowful. In His humanity, He prayed earnestly to His Father in heaven that He might not go through the ordeal, but ultimately affirmed that God's will must be done and not His.

"After going a little farther, He fell to the ground [distressed by the weight of His spiritual burden] and began to pray that if it were possible [in the Father's will], the hour [of suffering and death for the sins of mankind] might pass from Him. He was saying, 'Abba, Father! All things are possible for You; take this cup [of judgment] away from Me; but not what I will, but what You will.'"

[Mark 14:35-36 AMP]

Jesus prayed and asked God for something, as we do, but He said he wanted it only if it was possible and only if it was God's will. Jesus was with God before the foundations of the world when this plan was put in place, so He knew there was no other way. So profound was His trust in God that, regardless of the pain He knew He would suffer, He was still willing to go through with it.

Everything He did was according to the will of the Father. Had the Father decided to release Jesus from this task, Jesus would not have fulfilled His purpose, and where would we be? Jesus had to go through the suffering and the pain for us. He went on to conquer death, to rise from the grave and to come out greater than when He went in.

"Just consider and meditate on Him who endured from sinners such bitter hostility against Himself [consider it all in comparison with your trials], so that you will not grow weary and lose heart."

[Hebrews 12:3 AMP]

The message here is that we must go through hostile situations but remain focused on Jesus and what He went through, so as not to be discouraged. Jesus went through so much more than we ever will.

Our trials will be with us daily, and if we desire to follow in Jesus' footsteps, we must put aside our personal pleasures, take up these daily challenges, and follow Him.

"Then Jesus said to His disciples, 'If anyone wishes to follow Me [as My disciple], he must deny himself [set aside selfish interests], and take up his cross [expressing a willingness to endure whatever may come] and follow Me [believing in Me, conforming to My example in living and, if need be, suffering or perhaps dying because of faith in Me].'"

[Matthew 16:24 AMP]

Our faith in God must be absolute so that if we have to suffer, we should not think that our prayers have not been answered. Listen when He speaks to you; listen when He tells you that you have to go through suffering to develop a spiritual backbone and that you will be strengthened by the experience. Listen when He says, 'This is your time. I am bringing you home to be with me.' Believe that He is making the right decision for you and know that He has sent His angels to watch over you, just as He did with Jesus. God sent angels to encourage Jesus and to keep Him strong:

"Then the devil left Him; and angels came and ministered to Him [bringing Him food and serving Him]."

[Matthew 4:11 AMP]

God is facing your suffering with you because He will never leave you. Just because you didn't get the answer you wanted, when you wanted it, does not mean God has failed you.

TAKE NOTE

Your faith does not lie in what you ask for, it lies in the complete belief and trust in God to deliver according to His perfect will for your life.

If by faith you have asked God for something, don't assume that your request has been granted just because you asked for it. You will know when you have received it because you will have some confirmation such as total peace in your spirit or a dream or vision. Many of us have prayed for loved ones to be healed or not to die, but they were not healed and they did die, whilst others were healed and lived. God does not want us to be sick, but while some people receive healing, others do not. Ask yourself, if God healed all our sicknesses and prevented all our loved ones from dying, what was the point in Jesus' coming? Surely then this world would be perfect again and we would live forever, here and now.

If you did not receive the answer you were expecting and don't understand why, please talk to God. The Lord knows His plans for you, and they are greater than you could imagine, but it is always according to His will and not your own.

The Fear of God

There are times when you may be afraid of talking to God, scared that He may not answer or scared that He may be angry with you about something or other. You may think that He won't hear you because you don't deserve to be heard. This is not true! These feelings of fear and doubt are unfounded. Remember, salvation is for everyone and that includes you. God has given everyone direct access to Him.

Fear is a by-product of sin; it does not come from God. When Adam and Eve sinned for the first time in the Garden of Eden, their first negative emotion was a feeling of shame at realising they were naked. They immediately covered themselves with fig leaves to hide their shame. The second emotion they felt was fear, which made them hide from God when He came to see them. The God of the universe put time aside to come down to Earth to spend quality time with Adam and Eve, and they hid from Him because they were now affected by fear of what would happen as a result of their disobedience.

People often confuse their personal feelings of fear with the term 'to fear God'. The emotion of fear can be debilitating and should not go unchecked, but the fear of God is not to be confused with being afraid. To fear God is to have a deep awareness of who God really is, His greatness, and to live by His standard. It is to know that God is far more awesome and great than we could ever imagine. Having the fear of God in you is to have reverence for God and to live your life according to His teachings. Cornelius, a centurion in the Roman army, was "a devout man and one who feared God with all his household, who gave donations generously to the people, and prayed to God always" [Acts 10:2 – NKJV]. So, Cornelius' fear of God was apparent in the way he lived. He lived a life of prayer, active kindness and great devotion to God and was not afraid to pray to God or afraid of having a relationship with Him. And not just Cornelius, but his household.

To fear God is not to be afraid of God, so go to Him, talk to Him, spend time with Him and build your relationship with Him.

Be blessed!

Recommended Reading

1 Peter Chapter 1	Purpose in Christ
Galatians Chapter 5	Living by the Holy Spirit

ACTIVITY 6

What is your purpose? If you don't know, how can you find out?....

....

....

....

What strategies will you put in place to be a game-changer?............

....

....

Which attribute(s) of the Fruit of the Holy Spirit do you struggle with?..

....

....

How will you change this? ....

....

....

List the nine attributes of the Fruit of the Spirit. ....

....

....

Notes: ....

....

....

....

....

....

Finding Purpose in A Hurting World

This world we call home is all we know
The flowers bloom and the trees grow
The waters flow, streams, rivers and seas
And we feel the effects of the gentle breeze
Glistening stars in the sky at night
With the moon bringing forth its calming light
The warmth and brilliant glow of the sun
All affecting changes in our emotions
The beauty of the Earth cannot be denied
But its life and soul has ironically died.

Surely there must be something we can do
Make new laws and policies to undo
The damage and the sickness we try to conceal
And implement changes to help us heal
A world where so many hurt
Then look to others to convert
From this to that with no real purpose
No direction, still losing focus
But all being in the same position
Unable to change this dismal situation.

Lives taken, hearts broken
Trust misused and love abused
The outward appearance seeming tranquil
Beneath the surface nothing fulfilled
Seeking and searching to replace
That hopeless feeling without a face
This cannot be my purpose in life
To live in misery and then to die
Stop this pain, let me rest in peace
No more consciousness, I want my world to cease.

This lie that has been fed into our consciousness
Is destructive and must not be allowed to infest
Who we are and what we can achieve
Greatness and eternal peace
If you have tried all that the world can offer
And yet you still have no future
There is ONE you have not considered
He never fails and will deliver
You out of the hands of hopelessness
Why not put Him to the test?

Taking your life will not stop the pain
Renewed consciousness you will regain
There will be no rest or the peace that you sought
But eternal unrest, losing the battle you fought
Because you believed in your own ability
And rejected the Gift of Eternity
His Name transcends all the world has to offer
There is none to compare to His healing power
'Jesus, save me,' is all you need to say
And watch your world change the moment you PRAY!

CHAPTER 7
THE HOLY BIBLE

"All Scripture is given by inspiration of God, and is profitable for doctrine, for reproof, for correction, for instruction in righteousness, that the man of God may be complete, thoroughly equipped for every good work."

2 Timothy 3:16-17 NKJV

I have mentioned often the importance of reading and studying the Bible throughout your Christian life. The Holy Bible is the sacred book that Christians live by. It is a spiritual book in which the Holy Spirit reveals everything we need to know about God. The Bible was written by men, who gained inspiration from the Holy Spirit revealing things to them.

The Bible is the most beautifully written book you will ever read! Yes, I am gushing and, although I am prone to bias, you cannot deny that sentences like "Our Father who art in heaven" and "blessed are the poor in spirit, for theirs is the kingdom of heaven" are beautiful and poetic and resonate with your spirit.

The Bible is unique and spiritually uplifting because it is a spiritual gift to us from God that feeds our spirit when we read it. To read and understand it is to love it, and it is not a once-in-a-lifetime read—you will want and need to read it again and again. It is inexhaustible if you allow the Holy Spirit to reveal the deeper revelations of Christ in its pages.

FACT

The Holy Bible is the world's best-selling and most widely distributed book with over six billion copies printed worldwide. It tops the bestseller list in the world every single year without fail. There is no other book like it.

Many non-Christians believe the Bible is just a storybook written by men. They also believe that the stories are fictional and reject them as truths. Every story in the Bible is a factual narrative, not just a 'good story'. It is our history book as well as our spiritual book.

The term 'Bible' was first used in A.D. 400 and originates from the Greek word *biblia*, meaning 'rolls' or 'scrolls', which were made from papyrus and were the primary writing material used by the Greeks at that time. The Bible, meaning 'Book of Books' or a 'Collection of Books', was written by many different scribes (writers of the time) under the inspiration and anointing of the Holy Spirit.

The scribes were highly educated literary men who supported the prophets and wrote as they were directed. The Bible, which did not exist as one single volume until the fourth century A.D., consists of sixty-six books divided into two main sections, the Old Testament and the New Testament.

The Testaments

The word *testament* is defined as a "written document that states a person's wishes of one's personal property after death" [source: www.yourdictionary.com]. It is a covenant (agreement or promise) between God and the human race. The Old Testament is the first section of the Bible and was originally written in Hebrew. However, some books of the Old Testament and some elements of the New Testament are recorded in Aramaic (the language that Jesus spoke): "Taking the child's hand, He said [tenderly] to her, 'Talitha kum!'—which translated [from Aramaic] means, 'Little girl, I say to you, get up!'"

[Mark 5:41 AMP]

"And at the ninth hour Jesus cried out with a loud voice, 'Eloi, Eloi, lama sabachthani?'—which is translated, 'My God, My God, why have You forsaken Me?'"

[Mark 15:34 NKJV]

The vast majority of the New Testament, however, was written in Greek, the common everyday language of that time. The Old Testament or Old Covenant contains thirty-nine books (forty-six for Catholics and Orthodox denominations), starting with Genesis and ending with Malachi. Some of these books were written during the time between the Old and New Testaments, when God was 'silent' in the Earth. These books were not inspired by the Holy Spirit, so they have not been included in many versions of the Bible. They are known as the Apocrypha and are not part of the Hebrew Scriptures.

Apocrypha, as defined by Merriam-Webster, is writings or statements of dubious authenticity. These books are included in the Septuagint and Vulgate but excluded from the Jewish and Protestant canons (laws and principles) of the Old Testament. The Septuagint is the ancient Greek translation of the Jewish scriptures and the Vulgate is an early 5th-century version of the Bible in Latin, often called the 'Latin Vulgate'.

There are five main sections of the Old Testament. The first section contains the first five books of the Bible and is called 'Torah', which means 'Law' in Hebrew. In Greek it is called the 'Pentateuch', which means 'five books'. The first five books of the Bible were written by Moses and record the law of God as given to him to be taught to the Hebrews. The second section contains 'The Writings or Narratives', the third section is the 'Wisdom Literature', and the Old Testament ends with the 'Major Prophets' and 'Minor Prophets'.

The New Testament or 'New Covenant' is divided into four main sections, starting with the 'New Testament Narratives', which are the four gospels—meaning the Good News. The second section consists of 'Epistles by Paul', epistles meaning letters, the third section is the 'General Epistles', and the fourth is the 'Apocalyptic Epistle' by John. This is not John the Baptist, but John who was a disciple of Jesus and later became an Apostle.

Table 1 - Books of the Old Testament

	The Law or Torah	20	Proverbs
1	Genesis	21	Ecclesiastes
2	Exodus	22	Song of Solomon
3	Leviticus		**Major Prophets**
4	Numbers	23	Isaiah
5	Deuteronomy	24	Jeremiah
	Old Testament Narratives	25	Lamentations
6	Joshua	26	Ezekiel
7	Judges	27	Daniel
8	Ruth		**Minor Prophets**
9	1 Samuel	28	Hosea
10	2 Samuel	29	Joel
11	1 Kings	30	Amos
12	2 Kings	31	Obadiah
13	1 Chronicles	32	Jonah
14	2 Chronicles	33	Micah
15	Ezra	34	Nahum
16	Nehemiah	35	Habakkuk
17	Esther	36	Zephaniah
	Wisdom Literature	37	Haggai
18	Job	38	Zechariah
19	Psalms	39	Malachi

Table 2 - Books of the New Testament

New Testament Narratives			
40	Matthew	54	1 Timothy
41	Mark	55	2 Timothy
42	Luke	56	Titus
43	John	57	Philemon
44	Acts (of the Apostles)	**General Epistles**	
Epistles by Paul		58	Hebrews
45	Romans	59	James
46	1 Corinthians	60	1 Peter
47	2 Corinthians	61	2 Peter
48	Galatians	62	1 John
49	Ephesians	63	2 John
50	Philippians	64	3 John
51	Colossians	65	Jude
52	1 Thessalonians	**Apocalyptic Epistle by John**	
53	2 Thessalonians	66	Revelation

I have mentioned throughout this book that, as a new Christian, you must devote time to reading and studying the Bible. It is so important to do this because the Bible teaches us about the three persons of God, how to live a righteous life in Christ, how to pray and how to have a close relationship with God. It strengthens us when we are weak and it is food for our spirit. In short, the Bible is spiritual food for the Christian.

It is good to spend some time learning the books of the Bible and where they are located, as all too often during worship when the congregation is asked to turn to a specific book and chapter, many people are bewildered and a little lost. Sometimes they find it at the end of the reading and other times they don't find it at all, and this can be very frustrating and embarrassing for a new Christian. I have heard it said that Christians don't need to read the Old Testament because it is the old covenant and we only need to know about the new covenant. My immediate question to that is, why then did the Holy Spirit inspire men to write it and include it in the Bible?

Whilst it is true that we are under a new covenant, the covenant of grace brought to us by Jesus Christ, it is completely incorrect to think that we do not need to study the Old Testament. The Old Testament charts the beginning of mankind, it is the foundation of life and the history of our people. It provides us with the foundation of our faith. We must know where we came from and where we are going. The Old Testament is a rich legacy for the Christian, so please don't ignore it.

The plan of God has been continuous from its inception to now, being first revealed to us in the Old Testament with a small rest before the arrival of the New Testament.

Differences Between the Testaments

There were approximately four hundred years between the prophet Malachi, the last book of the Old Testament, and Matthew, the first book of the New Testament. God was 'silent' during this time, so the writings of this period were not inspired by the Holy Spirit. There were many battles and uprisings. The Jews were under Greek, then Roman control, and politically and religiously the world was ready for the coming of the Messiah, Jesus Christ.

Both testaments reveal the one true living God and the work of the three persons of the Godhead. The prophecies and revelation of Jesus Christ are contained in both testaments. Teachings on God's love, mercy, forgiveness, grace and redemption are the central foci of the Bible. Jesus is revealed in the scriptures from beginning to end.

The Old Testament charts the foundations of the Earth, the birth and the fall of mankind, and is often described as the New Testament concealed. It was also the dispensation (privileged time) of God the Father when He frequently visited the Earth. We see the heart of God and learn of His character. Many principles are established in this section of the Bible.

It contains prophecies of Jesus Christ, the Messiah (meaning The Promised Deliverer) both of the Jews and the world. It predicts events that continue to occur in this generation. It records the giving of God's Holy Law (the Ten Commandments and the ceremonial laws). We see God's anger against sin, with occasional glimpses of His grace. God primarily deals with the Jewish people and not so much the rest of the world.

The Passover and the holy festivals are instituted as well as the early covenants, which promised material blessings, such as land and cattle and earthly riches, along with heavenly legacies such as a heavenly king coming from the line of the Jewish king David, or the Gentiles (non-Jews) coming to know the Jewish God.

The New Testament is often described as the Old Testament revealed. It builds on the early foundations and principles with more revelations from God. Jesus fulfilled the prophecies of the Old Testament when He came and sacrificed Himself for us.

The primary foci of the New Testament are the person of Jesus Christ and The Holy Spirit. Prophecies and predictions in the Old Testament become New Testament truths. In this testament we see God's grace with the occasional glimpse of His judgement. Jesus fulfils the law, offers us grace and teaches us how to live by it. The law was given to show us that we could not succeed by our own efforts and that we needed a Saviour, Jesus Christ.

We learn how Jesus sacrificed Himself to save mankind and about the emergence of the Church. We see the workings of the

Holy Spirit, and there is great emphasis on spiritual blessings and heavenly riches rather than earthly material blessings.

The New Testament instructs the Christian in how to live a righteous life and fulfil their purpose in Christ.

Christians should aim to read the Bible on a daily basis, though it is not about how much you read, it's about how much you understand. A verse or two a day will be invaluable to you. Trying to read chapters at a time and not grasping the meaning can leave you frustrated. Whilst it is good to get excited about studying the Bible, be very careful not to get distracted with 'new fads' and practices and not to take the scriptures out of context. Do not get carried away with thinking you need to start learning Hebrew or Greek, start studying the original scrolls or resurrect Jewish feasts and practices. If you cannot understand the English version, how will you cope with the original Hebrew writings? It is a good idea to crawl, walk, then run; it won't work any other way.

Law vs Grace

Another impulse to avoid is the urge to start trying to live by Old Testament laws and practices. Jesus released us from these laws when He fulfilled every single one of them and brought the world under grace. "For out of His fullness [the superabundance of His grace and truth] we have all received grace upon grace [spiritual blessing upon spiritual blessing, favour upon favour, and gift heaped upon gift]. For the Law was given through Moses, but grace [the unearned, undeserved favour of God] and truth came through Jesus Christ."

[John 1:16-17 AMP]

If we ignore this and put ourselves back under law by trying to live by Old Testament rules, we are making what Jesus did for us redundant. Does this mean that we can do anything we want, break God's laws or live low moralistic lives? Absolutely not! It means we should not wake up every morning and be law-conscious, we should wake up and be grace-conscious. If you wake up today saying, 'I must keep the Ten Commandments,' you have already failed, and these are just a few reasons why:

First, you only have to break one law to be guilty of them all, so it's a tall order. You may say you are not a murderer or you do not steal, and that is fine, but what about adultery? Have you ever lusted or dreamed about someone in your heart or mind who is already married? What about your favourite celebrities, strangers or work colleagues? Just for a moment, even?

Jesus says, if we do this in our hearts, we have already committed adultery whether we follow through with the physical act or not. What about those little lies that we do not consider to be lies, or the ones by omission, or those to save someone else's feelings? A lie is a lie, great or small, regardless of the reason for it. Have you ever shouted at or disrespected your parents, left the room while they were talking or advising you and you didn't want to hear it, or disobeyed them? *No big deal*, you thought at the time, but respecting your parents is a big deal to God.

"If, however, you are [really] fulfilling the royal law according to the Scripture, 'You shall love your neighbour as yourself [that is, if you have an unselfish concern for others and do things for their benefit]' you are doing well. But if you show partiality [prejudice, favouritism], you are committing sin and are convicted by the Law as offenders. For whoever keeps the whole Law but stumbles in one point, he has become guilty of [breaking] all of it. For He who said, 'Do not commit adultery,' also said, 'Do not murder.' Now if you do not commit adultery, but you murder, you have become guilty of transgressing the [entire] Law."

[James 2:8-11 AMP]

So, to even show partiality to someone is failing in the law. If we all assessed ourselves anywhere near God's standard, we would find that we fail on a daily basis. Under the law, the punishment is severe and we would be guilty of breaking all laws, but under grace we are forgiven.

Who does not want forgiveness? No one can keep the law of God by their own efforts, and to say you can is to say that you are on the same level as Jesus, because He is the only one who could. By saying you have kept the Ten Commandments, you are breaking the one that says you should not lie, because you are lying. You cannot keep the laws, because if anyone could, God would not have sent Jesus Christ.

Pride is a sin that God cannot tolerate, so the moment you say you are keeping the Ten Commandments or you have kept

God's laws by your own efforts, you are saying you don't need Jesus' grace. This shows a huge amount of pride, which has no place in the righteous mind.

By now you are probably asking why God gave mankind these laws in the first place. Good question, and the answer is simple: we were given these laws to show us God's standard, to have the chance to try to live up to this standard ourselves and to see that we could not do it by our own efforts, but that we needed a Saviour. We failed miserably!

The New Testament represents God's grace and teaches mankind how to live righteous and holy lives in God, with His help and His strength and not by our own efforts. He sent the Comforter, who is the Holy Spirit, to dwell within us, reminding us of who we are in Christ, strengthening us, teaching and guiding us. Having failed to keep the law by our own strength, God says you need help, you need a Saviour, you need the Comforter, you need ME. By saying, 'I keep the Ten Commandments and God's laws', you are saying, 'I don't need YOU!'

"Why, then, the Law [what was its purpose]? It was added [after the promise to Abraham, to reveal to people their guilt] because of transgressions [that is, to make people conscious of the sinfulness of sin], and [the Law] was ordained through angels and delivered to Israel by the hand of a mediator [Moses, the mediator between God and Israel, to be in effect] until the Seed [Jesus] would come to whom the promise had been made."

[Galatians 3:19 AMP]

To continue trying to keep the law by your own efforts is to deny Christ and refuse to come under His grace. For those of you who are determined to keep the law and think it is just the Ten Commandments, let me be the first to tell you that you are missing the mark. The Ten Commandments are just the beginning. These laws come under the 'moral law system', but we also have the civil and ceremonial law systems, which total six hundred and thirteen commandments. This is referred to as the Mosaic Law because God gave them to Moses for the people of Israel.

As a Christian, when we practice unforgiveness, judge others or level accusations at each other, we are putting ourselves under law.

When we try to keep the law, putting steps and processes in place by following man-made rules, we are putting ourselves back under the law and ignoring grace. Anything that is not of grace is of the law. As stated previously, there are no grey areas or shades with God. Grace or law, Jesus or man! If you are not sure what grace is, just look at The Fruit of the Spirit chapter again: love, joy, peace, gentleness, kindness, faithfulness, patience, longsuffering, temperance (self-control). These are the attributes of God, and if you are not growing in these characteristics, something is amiss.

The Sabbath

I cannot leave this topic without mentioning the Sabbath—the controversial commandment! Should we keep it? Should we not? Should we worship on Sunday or should it be on Saturday? Christians from different denominations continue to disagree on the observance of the Sabbath, debating whether they are worshipping on the right day or the wrong day and levelling all sorts of accusations at each other. To get caught up in this battle puts you back under the law with confusion thriving in the midst. God is not a God of confusion, so He is not in it with you. Let us just keep it simple. When God created the heavens and the earth, He did this in six days and rested on the seventh. He blessed the seventh day and made it holy:

"And by the seventh day God completed His work which He had done, and He rested [ceased] on the seventh day from all His work which He had done. So God blessed the seventh day and sanctified it [as His own, that is, set it apart as holy from other days], because in it He rested from all His work which He had created and done."

[Genesis 2:2-3 AMP]

The Sabbath is rooted in the scripture above, God's holy gift to mankind. The Sabbath was instituted under the Mosaic Law, although it was observed in one form or another before this time. God created the Sabbath for 'man':

"Jesus said to them, 'The Sabbath was made for man, not man for the Sabbath. So the Son of Man is Lord even of the Sabbath [and He has authority over it].'"

[Mark 2:27-28 AMP]

The religious leaders of the time were very critical of Jesus as He went through the grain fields with His disciples plucking heads of grain on the Sabbath, the holy rest day. Jesus also healed on the Sabbath and this was apparently unlawful also.

In reality, religious leaders had changed the real meaning of the Sabbath through the years, turning it into a chore rather than a blessing. The Sabbath was given to us out of love, so as to avoid working ourselves into the ground; to rest and enjoy being in the presence of God, in worship and fellowship. But from being a blessing, it became man trying to live by God's standard again, another law we could not keep by our own efforts because life always got in the way, as Jesus showed us.

During the time between the testaments, Jewish religious leaders took it upon themselves to add additional rules and laws to the Sabbath to control the people, putting punishments in place should anyone break these rules. This changed the real significance of the gift of love from God and the Sabbath became more of a burden than a joy.

The Jewish Sabbath is held from Friday evening through to Saturday evening. When Christ died, He rose on Sunday, which is the first day of the week in the Gregorian calendar. This day is called the Lord's Day, and of course, Jesus is the Lord of the Sabbath, as He tells us from His own mouth. Christianity only came into being after Jesus arose and the Apostles planted the first churches of the New Testament. They preached, worshipped and broke bread on Sunday—the first day of the week.
"Now on the first day of the week, when the disciples came together to break bread, Paul, ready to depart the next day, spoke to them and continued his message until midnight."

[Acts 20:7 NKJV]

Those practising Judaism celebrate the Sabbath according to their laws, but the Christian follows Christ; we do not practise Judaism. The birth of Christianity saw the very first message being preached on a Sunday, so our day of worship is on Sundays. God still wants His people to rest in Him, whether this is on the Saturday or the Sunday. He does not expect us to remember all the commandments or find our own ways of keeping them. God's laws are now written in our hearts through His Holy Spirit; we are now led by Him who tells us how to live right.
"And the Holy Spirit also adds His testimony to us [in confirmation of this]; for after having said,

'This is the covenant that I will make with them
After those days, says the Lord:
I will imprint My laws upon their heart,
And on their mind I will inscribe them [producing an inward change],'
He then says,
'And their sins and their lawless acts
I will remember no more [no longer holding their sins against them].'
Now where there is [absolute] forgiveness and complete cancellation of the penalty of these things, there is no longer any offering [to be made to atone] for sin."

[Hebrews 10:15-18 AMP]

Here are a few facts to keep in mind when someone brings the Sabbath day argument to you:

- Where the Lord has taken away your sin, you are no longer expected to give an offering to remove that sin; it has already gone!
- The law was to compensate for our wrongdoings, our sin.
- Grace has now replaced law.
- The Holy Spirit will lead us into all truths.
- The Sabbath is now so much more than just one day; it is a godly way of life. It is resting in Jesus Christ every day of our Christian lives.
- It is that rest and peace and joy that we have in our lives regardless of what we are doing and what is happening around us.
- We do not have to wait for one day of the week to worship God, because we should live a life full of worship.

Don't wait for Sunday to tell the Lord how much you love Him, or to sing a song of praise to Him, or to pray and fellowship with Him—do it every day. As a Christian you must know what is written in the pages of the Bible and understand it so that you will recognise false doctrines and practices that could lead you away from Christ and ultimately from your salvation.

Recommended Reading

2 Timothy Chapter 3	The Scriptures in Perilous Times
Hebrews Chapter 10	God's Laws in our Hearts

ACTIVITY 7

Why is the Bible so important to Christians? ....

....

List two differences between the Old and New Testaments: ....

....

....

Who wrote the Bible? ....

....

Why was the law given to mankind?..

....

....

Who brought the law and who brought grace? ....

....

Who is the Lord of the Sabbath?..

Notes: ....

....

....

CHAPTER 8
EQUAL YET UNIQUE

Everyone is created equal, but at the same time we are all unique in our own way. One example of this uniqueness is our learning style; we don't all learn in the same way. While studying the Bible is a must for Christians, many seem to struggle and so are content with hearing what someone else has to say about it. Some people don't understand the Bible, which was understandable when we only had the King James Version, with its added challenge of early modern English—beautiful and poetic though it is. However, we now have so many translations, such as the New King James Version (NKJV), New International Version (NIV), New Living Translation (NLT) and the Amplified Bible (AMP), to name a few. We also have women's, men's, children's and study Bibles, which make it even easier to understand the Word of God, so we no longer have any excuses. We even have audio versions to listen to!

Many years ago, the Bible was only available to the rich and educated in the land, and its first translations were not readily accessible to the masses. People died translating the Bible so we would have full access to it today. Don't let it be in vain!

When beginning to study the Bible, the first thing to address is your learning style. Reflect on the way in which you learn and process information.

Learning Styles

Name	Description	My Style(s)
Auditory	The auditory learner learns best through listening.	
Kinaesthetic or Tactile	The kinaesthetic or tactile learner learns best through hands-on and physical activities. They work best with models.	
Visual	The visual learner learns best through images and concepts like diagrams, charts and maps.	
Reading and Writing	The learner who learns best through reading and writing likes to make lists and notes, write things down, and is good at memorising information.	

Notes: ....

....

....

....

....

....

You may have one learning style or a combination of several different styles. Once you have identified your learning style by ticking the relevant box or boxes above, start researching which Bible would suit the way you learn and work out the best way to study it.

Today, the Bible is available in many different formats and mediums. It is available to listen to on CD, MP4 and other listening formats; to watch on DVD; to read, watch and listen to on apps downloadable on phones, laptops, iPads and other mobile devices. And, of course, we have the written Bible, available with colour images, illustrations and maps, study plans, explanations of concepts and notes sections to encourage the reader to be interactive. Never have we had such an array of Bibles available to us.

The Bible contains natural and spiritual meanings. The natural meanings (such as what was actually happening at the time) and historical facts are easy enough to understand. The spiritual meanings, however, can only be taught by the Holy Spirit, and if we don't know Him or refuse to ask Him to teach us, then how can we learn from Him? Remember, we are limited—God is not.

Having identified your learning style, and found the Bible most suitable to you, before you even open its pages let's do something you may never have considered doing before. If you have, we are on the same page. Say a simple prayer for help and understanding as you read. Are you struggling with prayer or not sure how to pray or who to pray to? We have that covered in Chapter 10, but for now a simple prayer to help with your understanding when reading the Bible will do. This could include thanksgiving to God for bringing you this far, for providing you with your Bible, and, now that you have it, for His help in reading and understanding it.

Prayer for Help When Reading the Bible
Father in heaven, I thank you for bringing me this far and blessing me with your Holy Bible.
Now I set my heart to learn what is written in these pages. I pray that you will help me to understand your Word, and to reveal to me the deeper meanings of God.
I ask this in the name of my Lord and Saviour, Jesus Christ.
Amen.

Making A Start

I find the best starting point is Jesus. Everything starts and ends with Him, so the first book of the New Testament, Matthew, is where I encourage new Christians to start reading and studying. For anyone wanting to know about Jesus who has no terms of reference, this is a good starting point for them also. Part of knowing your learning style also involves knowing whether you enjoy reading or listening; going from start to finish in sequence, a chapter at a time; or whether you prefer topical studies, working on a particular subject regardless of whether the scriptures are in sequential order or not. No one can tell you your best way of studying; you need to assess this yourself. Some people can barely put the Bible down and read it cover-to-cover very quickly; others want to take everything in and read only a few verses a day.

Whichever way works best for you, it is strongly advised that you try to study the whole Bible at some point in your Christian life. It doesn't have to be in a linear way, but if you don't study it all, how will you know what you've missed? The point I am making here is that if you were reading another book, you would go from the beginning to the end and, although the Bible is not just any book, there is a lot to take in and understand, and you will never truly know what's in it if you refuse to study entire sections. God wants us to have the full knowledge of what is written in the Bible and there are consequences when we don't.

"My people are destroyed for lack of knowledge."

[Hosea 4:6 – NKJV]

Not studying the Bible causes problems both in the church and in society. People who don't understand the scriptures take them out of context and many new religious groups are created as a result of this. If someone reads part of the Old Testament and there is a further revelation of that scripture in the New Testament, if you never read the New Testament and cross-reference the scriptures, you will never know this. Some Christians disagree on the meaning of certain scriptures and, if you ask them, they will tell you only about one or two verses but not the scripture in its entirety.

If Christians do not read, study and understand the scriptures, they won't recognise the signs of the times, won't know how to live righteous lives and won't know how to survive and 'stand strong' in the face of adversity. We are encouraged in the following scripture to:

"Study to show yourself approved unto God, a workman that need not to be ashamed, rightly dividing the word of truth."

[2 Timothy 2:15 KJV]

In studying the Bible, we need not be ashamed and should use it in all areas of our life. We should never be embarrassed to share it, teach it and live by it. The Word of God is food for your spirit; when you read the Bible, it will strengthen you in your faith, teach you about God and teach you how to pray. Absolutely everything you need to know as a Christian is contained in this book.

You cannot be a game-changer without knowing the Word of God. There has to be a reason it outsells every other book ever written and continues to do so year after year. The power of the Bible will work in our lives if we let it. In some countries, people are killed for having a Bible and for their faith. Bibles have to be smuggled in by bold men and women of God born for this purpose. We are blessed (not lucky, the Christian does not believe in luck) not to be persecuted for possessing a Bible in the United Kingdom. Many men and women have died through the ages in their fight to make it accessible to everyone, from the king on the throne to the man in the field. Let us embrace this gift from God and use it.

You will not understand everything you read, so have your notebook, pen and Bible dictionary ready. Make notes and write down any questions you have. The Holy Spirit is your teacher first and foremost; if you ask Him, He will reveal the meaning of the scriptures to you. God has also given us teachers and leaders to help us, so don't be afraid to ask for their help. No question is too silly—if it is important to you, then it is important. There are also Bible forums on the internet, and teachings from some of the global teaching ministries. A word of caution, though—there are also many incorrect teachings on the internet and not everything that is backed up by a scripture is necessarily accurate. Please do ask the Holy Spirit for guidance and check the information with your church leaders and teachers. Make a note of questions until you can get answers for them.

Read a little every day. If you are not able to manage this, don't start feeling guilty and don't try to read twice as much to catch up. You will miss the point of studying and get yourself caught up in useless condemnation. If you are not able to read, then listen to it or watch it on DVD. It is important that you work at your own speed and your own understanding. The following table is a recommendation of which books of the Bible to study in your first few years in the Lord.

New Christian Study Plan

Books of the Bible	Summary	Start/ Completed Date
Matthew	• The life of Jesus, from birth through to death and resurrection.	
Mark	• The life of Jesus, from birth through to death and resurrection.	
Luke	• The life of Jesus, from birth through to death and resurrection.	

John	• The life of Jesus with a greater explanation of His divinity, that of Jesus as the Son of the living God and as God.	
Genesis	• The creation and fall of mankind • God's creative power • God's early Covenants • The call of God and the Patriarchs • The Prophets and our legacy	
Acts	• The power of Jesus Christ through the Holy Spirit • The power of Christ in the Apostles • The emergence of Christianity and the first church	

Psalms	• Strength and guidance when going through emotional struggles • Inspirational and uplifting teachings • Expressions of praise and worship to God	
Exodus	• God's ultimate power displayed • Freedom of God's people from bondage • God gives the Law to Moses • Living by the Law • Institution of the Holy Festivals	
Galatians	• Explanation of law vs grace • Why we are now under grace and what this means for the Christian	

Ruth	• A Journey of faith	
Romans	• The Christian's journey of faith • How to live a Christian life	
Esther	• Complete faith and determination	
1 & 2 Samuel	• The call of God • Obedience to God • God's love and protection for His people	
1 & 2 Corinthians	• The Christian life • Love • Spiritual Gifts	
Daniel	• Fasting, prayer, waiting on the Lord • How God delivered messages to His people • Prophecies for the future	

Revelation	• Past, present and future prophecies and revelations • The tribulation period • Christ's second coming • Judgement • The new heaven and the new earth	

If you reach the end of your first year as a Christian and have not read as much as you had hoped for, just keep going. Remember, life does not slow down to accommodate you and your learning; you have to be determined and focused. There will be time constraints, work, family and church commitments, so you must manage your time well. Make your Bible study time a priority. Don't say to yourself, 'I'm busy, God will understand.' Let's not take advantage of His mercy.

The Bible is here to help us, not God. We are the ones who need it, not Him. Don't get into the habit of putting everything ahead of God, and then justifying it because He is not standing in front of you pointing a finger with a disapproving look. When the devil tempted Jesus, he used flattery and tried to encourage Jesus to use His power for self-gratification. Jesus used the Word of God to chase him away, and we too must do this—but first we need to know it.

"Then the devil said to Him, 'If You are the Son of God, command this stone to turn into bread.' Jesus replied to him, 'It is written and forever remains written, "Man shall not live by bread alone".'"

[Luke 4:3-4 AMP]

Nothing else will feed the spirit man more than reading and studying the Bible continuously throughout your Christian life. Studying the Bible aids spiritual growth and gives you clarity when making decisions, peace in tumultuous situations and a real joy in your life. There will be times of peace and times of spiritual warfare. During times of peace, read and study well, for during times of warfare you will need the offensive weapon of the scriptures, also known as the Sword of the Spirit (see below). When we are in spiritual warfare, we must know how to use the sword to reject the enemy and protect ourselves and our loved ones.

Spiritual warfare is the battle the devil brings to us by trying to make us reject Jesus and lose our salvation. Many people who don't understand or accept that such a thing exists will refer to it as speculation and fiction. The devil will try to convince us of things that are not true and surround us with people who encourage wrong behaviour. He can possess and oppress a human being at will, he respects no one, and he does not ask permission before bringing the war to them. We were not created to be possessed, so this is never a good state for a human being to be in.

Possession is when demonic spirits (spirits sent from Satan) dwell within you and take over your will, control your thoughts and cause you to behave in ways counter-productive to you and others around you. Sometimes the person is aware of this and sometimes they are not. The person can become depressed, paranoid, fearful, anxious, self-destructive and harmful to themselves and others.

Satan can terrorise you in your sleep with nightmares and convince you that you are something when you are not. Having said all this, he cannot possess a <u>true</u> Christian filled with the Holy Spirit and completely surrendered to God, because he cannot withstand the power of the Holy Spirit who protects us. Note I said a Christian who is fully surrendered to God and has a real relationship with Him.

If as a Christian you refuse to fully surrender everything to God—live one way publicly and another privately, refuse to let go of certain worldly pleasures or a certain way of life—then you can provide a way in for the enemy to possess or oppress you.

Oppression is when the enemy sends demonic spirits to constantly urge you to sin and go against God's will. They do not possess from inside or control your will, they work from outside of the person, but both oppression and possession are extremely damaging, sometimes even fatal. The physical symptoms can include depression, mental instability, anxiety, stress, self-harm, extremely erratic and compulsive behaviour, and can manifest in the same way as someone who is possessed.

This happens a lot more often than the world realises and more often than we care to admit. There are many unexplained atrocities and heinous crimes committed in our world. Can you imagine what would happen if the perpetrator stood in front of the judge and said, 'Your honour, I did do the crime for which I am accused, but I was possessed at the time and had no willpower to stop myself'? Or, 'I am convinced I was oppressed by demonic spirits, because that was completely out of character for me'? Before they'd finished speaking they would be led out of the courtroom and sectioned with a plea of insanity entered on their behalf. One thing is clear: if this happens to you, you cannot win this battle on your own, you need help. Try Jesus. If you are already in the Lord, something has gone very wrong and you need to cry out to Him to help you and get help from your leaders or fellow Christians who can identify the seriousness of the situation.

Spiritual Weapons

As in any war, you need to armour up to protect yourself using your defensive weapons, and be ready to strike when necessary with your offensive weapons. This is not a physical battle, it is a spiritual one, so your weapons are spiritual and you need to be ready at all times. Prepare for the unexpected!

Your Spiritual Weapons [Ephesians 6]:

1. Knowing the <u>Truth</u> of Jesus Christ
2. Living a <u>Righteous</u> life
3. Knowing how to live, and living, a <u>Peaceful</u> life
4. Having great <u>Faith</u> in God and exercising it
5. Receiving <u>Salvation</u>; to be saved

} Defensive Weapons to ward off the attacks

6. Knowing the <u>Word of God</u> by studying the Bible and using it when necessary—the Sword of the Spirit

7. <u>Praying</u> always to activate God's power to work on our behalf

} Offensive Weapons when we need to attack

The Bible is our greatest weapon and our first port of call. Download it on your mobile devices, carry a hard copy in your bag, and listen to it on your audio devices. However you do it, just make sure you study it. Put time aside, and be single-minded and focused. If it is that important to you and you desire it, you will find time to study it.

"For the word of God is living and active and full of power [making it operative, energising, and effective]. It is sharper than any two-edged sword, penetrating as far as the division of the soul and spirit [the completeness of a person], and of both joints and marrow [the deepest parts of our nature], exposing and judging the very thoughts and intentions of the heart."

[Hebrews 4:12 AMP]

We need to be great swordsmen and women of God and know how to use these spiritual weapons!

Recommended Reading

Make a start on the new Christian Bible study plan.

ACTIVITY 8

What's the best starting point when beginning to study the Bible, and why?..

....

....

....

Why should you study the Bible? ....

....

....

How many Testaments are there in the Bible? Name them:..............

....

....

List five of your spiritual weapons:...

....

....

Where in the Bible will you find a list of your spiritual weapons? ...

....

Notes: ....

CHAPTER 9
HOW RELEVANT IS THE BIBLE TODAY?

As you travel on your journey, you will hear strange comments like 'the Bible is not relevant for these times' and 'we need something new to deal with today's challenges'. The Bible is the most accurate history of the world and prophetic book that's ever been printed—nothing else comes close. The Bible is so advanced and future-proof that many choose to deny this, only to try to prove their own theories. The pages of this book cannot contain all the arguments against those theories, so I will highlight just one.

Jesus told us about the signs of the times and the end of the age over two thousand years ago. In the following scripture, make a note of all the things you are aware of that are either happening in the world at this very moment or have happened already. This is how accurate and relevant the Bible is today.

"They asked Him, 'Teacher, when will these things happen? And what will be the sign when these things are about to happen?' He said, 'Be careful and see to it that you are not misled; for many will come in My name [appropriating for themselves the name Messiah which belongs to Me alone], saying, "I am He," and, "The time is near!" Do not follow them. When you hear of wars and disturbances [civil unrest, revolts, uprisings], do not panic; for these things must take place first, but the end will not come immediately.'

Then Jesus told them, 'Nation will rise against nation and kingdom against kingdom. There will be violent earthquakes, and in various places famines and [deadly and devastating] pestilences [plagues, epidemics]; and there will be terrible sights and great signs from heaven.

'But before all these things, they will lay their hands on you and will persecute you, turning you over to the synagogues and prisons, and bringing you before kings and governors for My name's sake. This will be a time and an opportunity for you to testify [about Me]. So make up your minds not to prepare beforehand to defend yourselves; for I will give you [skilful] words and wisdom which none of your opponents will be able to resist or refute. But you will be betrayed and handed over even by parents and brothers and relatives and friends, and they will put some of you to death, and you will be continually hated by everyone because of [your association with] My name. But not a hair of your head will perish. By your [patient] endurance [empowered by the Holy Spirit] you will gain your souls.'"

[Luke 21:7-18 AMP]

Things currently happening in the world today as identified in this scripture: ....

....

....

....

....

....

....

....

....

....

....

....

....

....

....

....

....

....

....

....

....

....

The Parable of the Sower

The Parable of the Sower is a very good scripture for new Christians to study and understand. It will help you to identify where you are on your Christian journey. Jesus taught the multitudes in parables (short stories) to help them to understand the points He was making. When we come to the Lord, we hear the Word of God through preaching and teachings, but do we really take it in and live by it?

As explained previously, we do not all process information in the same way and we are not all affected by what we hear in the same way. There are many variables that dictate the way in which a person receives and processes the Word of God:

- Our current and past circumstances
- Our experiences
- The way we think

- Our belief systems
- How easily we are influenced by others
- The type of influences we are surrounded by
- To what extent we are truly surrendered to the Lord
- How much of the world we are still trying to hold onto
- The support network we have around us

The list goes on…

In the following parable Jesus outlines the four states a person may find themselves in when they hear the Word preached.

"He told them many things in parables, saying, 'Listen carefully: a sower went out to sow [seed in his field]; and as he sowed, some seed fell beside the road [between the fields], and the birds came and ate it. Other seed fell on rocky ground, where they did not have much soil; and at once they sprang up because they had no depth of soil. But when the sun rose, they were scorched; and because they had no root, they withered away. Other seed fell among thorns, and thorns came up and choked them out. Other seed fell on good soil and yielded grain, some a hundred times as much [as was sown], some sixty [times as much], and some thirty. He who has ears [to hear], let him hear and heed My words.'"

[Matthew 13:3-9 AMP]

How the Parable of the Sower Applies to the Life of a Christian
The Sower

The Preacher or teacher who preaches or teaches the Word of the kingdom, which affects people's lives.

The Wayside

When someone hears the Word of the kingdom and does not understand it, then the wicked one comes and snatches away what was sown in their heart.

In the life of the Christian: You hear the Word of the kingdom but you don't understand it. You need to ask questions of your leaders and teachers, who are there to help. Regardless of how silly you may think the questions are, you need to ask them. You need to be proactive and read and study the Word for yourself, asking the Holy Spirit for deeper understanding. When Jesus died for you, He gave you direct access to God, so pray for **greater** understanding and you will receive it. There are also false teachers in the world, and only by knowing the Word for yourself will you know if the teachings you are receiving are the same as what are written in the Bible. You have to fight for what you believe in. It is a learning curve for all of us, without exception!

Stony Places

When someone hears the Word and immediately receives it with joy, he has no root in himself, but his joy lasts only for a while. For when tribulation or persecution arises because of the Word, immediately he stumbles.

In the life of the Christian: You hear the Word, you love it, and you receive it immediately, but do you really believe it? The Word tells us that we will be challenged and persecuted, but when this happens you become angry, feel hopeless and begin to struggle with your faith. You become weak because you are not rooted, and you refuse to do what the Bible says you should do in these circumstances. Many Christians who are hurt by other Christians or religious practices often fall into this category. They are unable to forgive and move on with their Christian life and often declare they will never go into another church again!

Among the Thorns

When someone hears the Word and the cares of this world and the deceitfulness of riches choke the Word, and he becomes unfruitful and does not grow spiritually.

In the life of The Christian: You hear and understand the Word, but you still want everything the world has to offer. You pray vain prayers, concerned with becoming rich in materialistic possessions, and are deceived into thinking it is sufficient for you. You are straddling the Kingdom of God and the Kingdom of Satan. You cannot have both. This is not to say that Christians cannot or should not be rich, but you can only maintain the right balance with God at the centre of it, so you do not worship your wealth. Many Christians who no longer have a relationship with God and have started doing it 'their way' fall into this category. You are not growing spiritually or doing the will of God, but you think you are. You have been deceived!

The Good Ground

When someone hears the Word and understands it, and indeed bears fruit: some a hundredfold, some sixty, some thirty.

In the life of The Christian: You have heard and accepted the Word. You are studying by yourself as well as through the teaching you receive. You are growing in your faith by applying the Word to your life. Keep going! The point is that you 'get it'. We will not all learn and understand at the same pace, so don't watch others, just keep going on your own journey. Whether you are growing at one hundred percent, sixty or thirty, you are on good ground, you are growing, your roots are deep and you are fruitful, so others can see you developing in your faith as a Christian should. Stay strong and be prepared for the unexpected.

***

When the seed was sown in your heart, where did it fall? Where are you in your Christian walk? The Parable of the Sower teaches us that there is only one ground the Christian should be on, and that is the good ground. There is no in-between or straddling across different grounds. The seeds that fall on the good ground are those who hear the Word of the kingdom and live by it.

Remember, the Bible is the 'Book of Books' and is made up of sixty-six books, so don't try to climb the mountain from the top by trying to read them more quickly than you can understand what you are reading, for it is like no other book. You need to start climbing the mountain from the bottom. Don't stop until you reach the top!

Recommended Reading

Luke Chapter 21	The Signs of the Times
Matthew Chapter 13	The Parable of the Sower

ACTIVITY 9

The Bible is not relevant in the 21st century. True or false?...............

....

In the Parable of the Sower, how many different grounds does the seed fall on?...

....

List four variables which affect how a person processes the Word of God:..

....

....

Which ground are you on? ....

....

....

How are you developing on your Christian journey?.........................

....

....

....

....

Notes: ....

....

....

....

....

....

....

The Beauty of The Word

On His Word we stand
The Holy Book penned by God's own hand
Inspired by His Holy Spirit
Written by those who truly lived it
Our history book of the ages
With precious teachings betwixt its pages
Charting the journey from beginning to end
Of a world which we cannot truly comprehend.

Book of Books, it is our daily bread
Newborn babes on its milk are fed
Feeding and strengthening our spirit being
Preparing us for the unseeing
Its fountain of knowledge we depend on
To frustrate the enemy's plans—let them be gone
In the Word is the power to create
Breaking down all that was built on hate.

All that we are and endeavour to be
It is the Word in the flesh who sets us free
The coming of Christ prophesied
Because God's Word cannot return void
His life, death and resurrection
Made free the gift of salvation
Grace and truth by Him were ushered in
And now we await His second coming.

Its spiritual meaning sometimes lost
As many attempt to quantify the cost
Of spending time in God's presence
Studying and learning with reverence
Not understanding that which is written
Anointed, blessed and Holy Spirit given
Preaching instead only what they've heard
But nothing can deny the beauty of His Word.

CHAPTER 10
WHAT IS PRAYER?

"Do not be anxious or worried about anything, but in everything [every circumstance and situation] by prayer and petition with thanksgiving, continue to make your [specific] requests known to God."

Philippians 4:6 AMP

Prayer is an alien concept to many. It is unthinkable to speak openly to someone you cannot see. A person who does not believe in anything, or is not sure what to believe in, will probably laugh nervously or look uncomfortable if you recommend prayer to them. The very thought of it will result in them feeling awkward, silly and confused. I mentioned prayer earlier in *The Best Journey Ever* and you probably reflected on your prayer life: whether you pray enough, if you are praying the right way, who you should be praying to and such like. Many new Christians see mature Christians praying publicly, quoting scriptures and praying in tongues (praying in the Spirit) and become nervous and unsure about their own prayer life, wondering about the right way to pray.

So what is prayer and how should we pray? Prayer, put simply, is the way in which we communicate with God by speaking to Him, praising Him and listening to Him when He speaks to us. Have you ever been in a relationship with someone without ever speaking to or communicating with them and ignoring them when they tried to communicate with you? How did that work out for you? No doubt it caused problems and unhappiness, leading to eventual breakdown and separation from that person. All parties are wounded and scarred from the experience and some are no longer able to trust anyone again. That's the usual pattern.

Communication is vastly underrated but so completely necessary. Bad communication is unquestionably a deal-breaker in relationships. It is the same in our relationship with God. We cannot have an effective relationship with Him if we do not communicate with Him, and we do this through prayer. Every Christian has direct access to God, which means we do not need a high priest to pray to God on our behalf or to ask God to forgive our sins, as was the case in the Old Testament. God directed Moses to select priests from the tribe of the Levites. The first priests were Moses' brother Aaron and Aaron's sons. They were the only people allowed into the Tabernacle of Meeting, where the altar of God was located behind the veil. This was the Holy of Holies, the most holy place where God's presence lived. Everything in there was anointed and made holy.

"With it you shall anoint the tabernacle of meeting and the ark of the Testimony; the table and all its utensils, the lampstand and its utensils, and the altar of incense…

And you shall anoint Aaron and his sons, and consecrate them, that they may minister to Me as priests."

[Exodus 30:26-30 NKJV]

The priests were anointed and blessed by Moses to make them holy so they could go into God's presence. Anyone with sin could not enter the Holy of Holies or touch anything in there or they would die, even the priests. So the priests would carry the weight of the sin committed by the people, and mediate between them and God. They would perform the sin offerings, burnt offerings and peace offerings to God for the sins of the people.

This all changed when Jesus died for us. He made it possible for every person to go to God for themselves and to be in His presence. Jesus' death removed the veil and all the obstacles. No one is required to go to God on our behalf, and we do not have to be perfect and sinless to go into His presence. Seeking the Lord in prayer with a repentant heart gives you access to enter the Holy of Holies, which is no longer a physical place but a spiritual one. You can talk to God about your sins, ask for forgiveness, fellowship with Him and find out directly from Him what His purpose for your life is. You and you alone are responsible for your relationship with God; no mediator other than Jesus is necessary.

The way we pray is different for everyone as we are all unique and express ourselves in different ways. Some people are very vocal, and can pray loudly and for hours, while others prefer to pray silently or in their hearts. Some Christians are very good at setting specific times to pray and some will pray throughout the day whenever they want to talk to God. The way you pray and your prayer life will develop as you spend time with the Holy Spirit and allow Him to teach you.

As Christians we should be imitators of Christ, aspiring to be like Him in all His ways, so a good starting point for your prayer life is to look at how He prayed. The religious establishment and the multitudes criticised Jesus relentlessly about everything, and one of the complaints was that He and His disciples did not pray and fast like them. They loved to be on show praying and fasting in public, to be seen by all and turn it into a spectacle. But Jesus teaches us how to pray:

"After He had dismissed the crowds, He went up on the mountain by Himself to pray. When it was evening, He was there alone."

[Matthew 14:23 AMP]

"Early in the morning, while it was still dark, Jesus got up, left [the house], and went out to a secluded place, and was praying there."

[Mark 1:35 AMP]

Jesus often prayed on His own, away from the public, on a mountain or in the wilderness, in the morning long before daylight, but he also prayed during the day and in the evening, before He ate or gave food to anyone. Jesus *lived* a life of prayer.

When necessary, but not often, He prayed in public, as He did just before He raised Lazarus from the dead [John 11:41-42], and He did this because the people needed to know that He was sent by God the Father and to glorify God, not for a personal show. Jesus prayed before He worked miracles. With the loaves of bread and the fish, He looked up to heaven and blessed the food before feeding the multitudes [Mark 6:41].

He prayed in private and did not allow anyone to distract Him until He was finished. The distractions were great as often multitudes, and even His disciples, were following and looking for Him.

There are many scriptures confirming that Jesus prayed throughout His life on Earth, so this tells us that prayer is extremely important in the life of a Christian. Jesus always led by example, and in *all* His prayers, He only ever prayed to God the Father. At no time did He ever address anyone else in His prayers: not the angels, nor His mother, nor any other beings. He always addressed the Father with reverence and respect and humbled Himself before Him, even though He is His Son. You don't have to shout or be aggressive when praying to the Lord, but you can be passionate and expressive and there are times when you will cry out to Him. It's never necessary to shout at the Lord to get Him to give you what you want when you want it. Making a joyful noise to the Lord in worship or crying out in praise, or in desperation even, is a different matter.

Father and Son were in communication all the time Jesus was on Earth and we too must be in communication with God all the time. It absolutely baffles me when I hear Christians saying that they don't pray as often as they should. I'm not really sure what that even means. What they are saying is that the God they serve, who is with them at all times, dwells within them, is with them when they sleep and when they wake, when they are eating, driving or watching the television, the God who is their best friend, is being ignored by them for days, weeks, months or just whenever they like! My answer to that is, 'If you are too busy to pray, you are definitely too busy.'

No one can say they are leading a busier life than Jesus did, or that they are more tired than He was, or that they are called for a greater purpose than He was. He had thousands of people following Him around at all times, not just when there was an organised monthly or annual event as is the practice of our modern churches. They cut a roof through the house that He was in to lower a sick man to be healed [Luke 5:19]; they found Him on the Sabbath; they found Him when He stepped out of His house in the morning, or whichever house He'd slept in the night before; and still He found time to pray! We have no excuse not to pray. If you can say that your purpose in life is to save the world and the billions of people in it, to journey between heaven, Earth and hell, to bring the demonic world under subjection, and more, then you have an argument for not praying—yet the One who did all those things prayed constantly.

The Christian needs to make time to pray. We all make time for the things we consider to be important, regardless of the commitments we already have in our lives. If you're a morning person, wake up before work and pray; if you are a night person, pray at the end of the day; if you are good at managing your day, then take time out during the day.

When a person is committed to someone or something they believe in and love, they will do whatever they need to do to build and nurture their relationship and that love. Dog owners will dash home from work in their limited lunch break to feed and walk their dogs; people who love to socialise will rush home from work, tired though they are, and shower, preen and prepare for the occasion before going out all night to enjoy themselves, arrive home in the early hours of the following morning, inebriated and exhausted, and get up bright and early for work the next day, repeating the pattern for the rest of their lives; a person who loves cars will allow a new car to take up much of their time and money in cleaning, polishing and maintenance. Why? Because they love it!

Christians, there are no excuses for not finding time to pray. No one needs to see or hear you praying and you don't have to kneel; God sees and hears you. Kneeling is a sign of humility and, when you humble yourself to God in your private time, this is between you and Him. Whether you sit, kneel, stand or lay down, it really doesn't matter. As a new Christian or someone who has never prayed before, start off by asking the Holy Spirit to teach you how to pray; He is our ultimate teacher and He will teach you to pray like Christ. In asking Him to help you, you are already communicating with God—remember He is God the Holy Spirit.

Baby Steps

Always keep it simple and don't complicate matters or confuse yourself. If you wake in the morning and your partner is lying next to you, the first thing you would say to that person, if you are communicating with each other, would be 'Good morning', so start with good morning! If you are feeling a little shy and uncertain about speaking to the Lord, why not start with, 'Good morning, Holy Spirit; good morning, Lord Jesus; good morning, my Father in heaven.' Take baby steps.

You've woken up. Many went to bed last night and didn't wake up, so thanks would be a natural progression: 'Thank you for waking me this morning.' You have a busy day ahead, or you are not sure what you will be doing for the day, so share that with Him: 'Lord, I have a difficult day ahead—please help me through it.' Add anything else you want to discuss with the Lord when you wake up. This is simply fellowshipping with God, having a conversation with Him, acknowledging His presence and giving Him thanks.

Once you start, the Holy Spirit will work with you to continue in prayer and it will become easier and more natural. You just need to keep it simple and speak from the heart. No rehearsals needed. Don't worry about Christian 'jargon' and trying to fashion your prayer according to how you see others pray. At this early stage in your Christian journey, when you are a 'babe in Christ', it is good to take baby steps and start by fellowshipping with the Holy Spirit. Acknowledge Him as He is always with you; don't worry about structure or duration, that will come later.

Tell the Lord what is on your mind. Yes, He knows already, but opening up to Him shows a surrendered heart and allows Him to teach you the things you need to learn. Although we do not need a mediator between us and God, we can ask for prayers or pray for others. The more we pray and spend time with God, the more we will know, understand and love Him. He already loves us, but the problem is our lack of love for Him.

When you pray, you should pray to the Father in the name of Jesus. You must never pray to angels, saints, objects, anyone else or anything. Only God can answer your prayers, so praying to anyone else is a waste of your precious time. If you do, you won't get an answer from God or the objects you pray to, but you may get an answer from the enemy—and you don't want that! In our prayer template, as mentioned earlier, Jesus teaches us to pray [Matthew 6:6-15]:

Our Father in heaven, Hallowed be Your name.	Always pray to the Father. Address Him with reverence and declare who He is.
Your kingdom come. Your will be done On Earth as *it is* in heaven.	Although you can ask the Lord for anything, it is granted according to His will and this should be acknowledged.
Give us this day our daily bread. And forgive us our debts, As we forgive our debtors.	Ask the Lord for what you need to sustain you daily and ask for His forgiveness for the things you've done wrong, but you also must forgive others at the same time.
And do not lead us into temptation, But deliver us from the evil one.	Acknowledge the challenges and temptations ahead and ask for protection and deliverance from the enemy's attacks.
For Yours is the kingdom and the power and the glory forever. Amen.	Acknowledgement and praise of God's power, giving Him all the glory due to Him. Seal your prayers with Amen, which means 'let it be so', or 'so be it'.

This prayer encompasses all the areas we should pray for on a regular basis, but you can vary it to suit your needs. We live in a society where, if you pray for someone with the intention of helping them, you could be met with hostility and, worse, taken to court to answer for your actions or even lose your job. It is often seen as an insult if you offer to pray for someone who does not believe in God. It can be misconstrued as forcing your beliefs onto someone else and they sometimes feel that you are trying to take their freedom of choice away from them. Life is a challenge, so these obstacles should not deter you from continuing to pray for others.

If you wish to pray for someone, you can do it privately or you can ask them. As Christians, we pray for anyone and everyone. We pray for countries, for leaders, the poor, the sick, our families, anyone suffering persecution, friends, strangers. Absolutely anyone laid on your heart to pray for, you should pray for them. This type of prayer is called intercessory (go-between) prayer. It is when you intercede on someone else's behalf by praying to God for them when they are not able to do it for themselves.

In John 17, verses 6-19, Jesus interceded to the Father for His disciples, and in verses 20-26, for all believers. To pray for someone is not to force your beliefs on them, it is to help them. You pray for people because you love them, whether you know them or not. It was because of that love that Jesus came to die for us and told us in turn to love each other. He prayed for us regardless of whether we gave permission or not.

Many do not believe in prayer, but when there are earthquakes or other forms of natural disaster where there is loss of life or potential loss of life, the churches are packed and people start asking for someone to pray for them. Suddenly people are willing to open their minds to the possibility of 'what if?', and this is a good thing and to be encouraged. Many start praying for the first time and pleading, 'God, if you are out there, please help me.' Then we have those at the other end of the spectrum asking, 'If there is a God, why did He let this happen?' If you don't believe there is a God, then the question is redundant.

If you knew God, you wouldn't ask that because you would be blaming Him for something that mankind, along with Satan, did a long time ago; we are in a fallen world which is literally breaking apart and we did this, not God.

Different Types of Prayer

There are different types of prayer for different situations, which you will learn about and build on as you grow in Christ:

- Prayer of Agreement
  - Christians in total agreement and praying for something specific
- Prayer of Consecration (meaning association with the holy, blessing, dedication)

- ○ Prayer to dedicate yourself to God's holy will
- ○ Prayer to bless or dedicate someone or something
- Corporate Prayer
  - ○ Believers praying in groups. Corporate prayers can be done on a global scale when details have been sent to everyone of what to pray for and when
- Prayer of Faith
  - ○ All prayers are by faith, for the Christian must live by faith
  - ○ The prayer of faith, however, is to make a specific reques to God with unusual requirements, which only someone with a great measure of faith would undertake
- Prayer of Intercession
  - ○ Praying for others, often referred to as 'standing in the gap'. Going to God on behalf of someone else
- Prayer of Petition
  - ○ A humble prayer of appeal to God pleading for something and putting your case to the Lord with reasons to strengthen your plea
- Praying in the Spirit
  - ○ Praying in the unknown tongue, your heavenly language, which every Christian can and should receive, as it is a promise from God. Not to be confused with the gift of tongues, which can be interpreted by others and may be a foreign language which you have never learned
- Ministering to God
  - ○ Worshipping God, giving Him praise and thanksgiving, talking and fellowshipping with Him
  - ○ Prayers where you are not asking anything of the Lord but are sharing and giving of yourself to Him

Start communicating with the Lord now. Pray any time of the day or night. When you wake up, in the shower, while you're travelling to or from work, when you're washing up, when you're relaxing on the sofa or in bed. Absolutely any time is the right time, and don't be too regimental with duration, location and physical positioning (i.e. kneeling, clasping your hands in front of you). The discipline will develop the more you pray, and your desire to pray will grow.

You are probably wondering about closing your eyes when you pray, and thinking, 'How can I do this when I'm travelling to and from work or doing the household chores?' You don't have to close your eyes when praying. We only do this to close out distractions and concentrate on our prayer. You can learn to pray with your eyes open or closed so you are ready for all eventualities. You can pray in your mind or out loud—there are times when you will do both.

Closing your eyes, bowing your head, clasping your hands and kneeling are all marks of humility and respect and can be done when you are in private. Many of these religious practices have evolved through the ages, but there are no scriptures requiring that the Christian must do these things when praying. Prayer is from the heart. It is the condition of the heart that the Lord will respond to, not regimental practices.

On the day of Pentecost, when the hundred and twenty prayed in the upper room and the Holy Spirit descended from the heavens and filled them, they were sitting.

"When the day of Pentecost had come, they were all together in one place, and suddenly a sound came from heaven like a rushing violent wind, and it filled the whole house where they were sitting."

[Acts 2:1-2 AMP]

Jesus taught us to pray the Lord's Prayer, and nowhere in it did He say lay on the floor, kneel, or any of those things. Let the Holy Spirit guide your heart and do what you are comfortable with. If in doubt, ask Him. Prayer is both beneficial and powerful.

The below testimony tells us how God answers prayers when we are determined to seek Him.

When you pray, put all your problems before God and ask Him to help you to overcome them. Put your enemies, your challenges and your struggles before God and ask Him to help you to get through them. But don't only go to God when you are sad or struggling—share your joys and your happiness also. Tell Him about your loved ones and pray for them to be saved if they are still in the world. Laugh with Him, cry to Him, and praise Him both when you are happy and when you are sad. In your darkest hour call out to Him and, if you don't know what to say, say nothing. He knows what you need to bring you through and to build you up. Tears are prayers also; He understands the language!

Watch Your World Change

When you start praying to God your world will change overnight, literally. You will find strength you didn't know you had, you will have clarity of mind, you will have a joy in your spirit even when you are sad, because that joy is in Christ. You will hear him clearly in your spirit, and you will make the right decisions in your life. In short, you will be victorious in Christ and this will frustrate the enemy. Remember, you are a game-changer!

In the following testimony, Shelley put this to the test the moment she came to Christ and proved God in her life.

Shelley's Testimony

I have always believed there is a God and there is a higher power that is beyond human comprehension. I looked at the beauty of the world at a young age and, without a shadow of a doubt, believed there was something beyond me. I was born into a Sikh family, following and practicing the Sikh religion. In my mid-teens I began to question religion, not able to understand why there were so many. If all religions believe there is one God, why were there so many different practices and differences in teachings? Surely there had to be the ultimate truth!

I turned away from my Sikh practices and I remember sitting in bed one day, at the age of 15, and speaking to God. I said, "I'm speaking directly to you, God, and since there is only one God I need you to tell me the truth." I had a Bible at the time that had been given to me from school and one day I began reading it; I couldn't stop. The more I read, the more I seemed satisfied, but couldn't understand why. I prayed and I prayed and couldn't understand at the time what was drawing me so much to find out about Jesus. I continued to search and I could feel my heart starting to change, genuinely change. My heart would begin to feel guilty when I did things wrong. I had never felt that way before. All the things I had tried so hard to shift were starting to move. I knew in my heart that God was leading me more and more towards understanding who He was.

I would sit night after night testing God through my prayers by asking questions, and He surely answered. I could see my circumstances changing around me. I had always been a very fearful person but, when I began praying, this fear gradually began to fade. I now had clarity, peace and contentment, all internal feelings that I had never felt before. What would my family and friends think? "I just believe in a God," was all I could say when the questions started coming.

It was a difficult time for me because I really wanted to fit in. My friends were all Indian and each year it was customary to celebrate Sikh holy days. I just couldn't continue to be involved in these religious practices anymore, and the pressure from my family grew. I began to make many excuses not to attend them but knew this could not continue indefinitely. I began attending church as my curiosity to know more grew.

Many believed I was 'brainwashed' and, ten years later, my family members are still convinced that I am. My mum is a Christian and my father is Sikh, and she too deals with many challenges from family and friends. My realisation of who God is required building a real relationship with Him, just between myself and Him, and this is where my focus lies.

Ten years later, I made the commitment to follow Jesus and was baptised into the Christian faith. The spiritual attacks against me because of my belief in Jesus Christ have been the most challenging experiences of my life, emotionally, mentally and spiritually. My relationships have failed, my friendships have failed, even my finances have been under attack, and the challenges at work almost cost me my job. Being in a relationship with someone who wasn't a Christian was emotionally draining because I was trying to please everyone and make them happy. It is the hardest thing for some people to fathom or accept when you have made a choice to follow the Lord. I'm still Indian, just with a heart for Christ and who no longer follows the Sikh religion.

It's not an easy walk. Some days I felt so low I couldn't even get out of bed. I remember feeling so low but knowing that God was the only one who could make me feel better, and He did. I started wondering what difference it would make to my daily life if I started spending more time with God, so I did. I began praying one evening *and, when I'd finished, one hour had gone by. I continued to pray daily, sometimes for thirty minutes, sometimes for an hour. I had not planned the times or duration, I just called on the Lord to help me and began to build a relationship with Him by talking to Him daily.*

I prayed a lot about my home life at the time as it was quite difficult. I would say, "God, you know my situation", and I would ask Him for scriptures which applied to my life and what I was going through at the time. I knew God was leading me because the scriptures were accurate every time. I felt so good after praying to God that I could have 'bounced off the walls'. My spirit had never felt so fulfilled and refreshed, so naturally I kept it up. It felt like there was a fire burning inside me, ready to explode, and I could distinctly feel and see the differences in my life. My circumstances started to change without me doing anything to change them. I was able to make difficult decisions in my job and relationships with confidence and clarity, where before I had been confused, uncertain and fearful. I could finally see the light at the end of the tunnel. God truly began to bless me as I spent more time with Him.

My spiritual life has never been so beautiful and fruitful. It came from one source alone and that was Jesus, Son of the Living God. I cannot truly tell you how powerful His name is; you really have to experience Him for yourself. I thank God daily for his grace and favour over my life. For those who don't know who God is or feel that there is no meaning to their life, my only advice is to try Jesus by speaking directly to him.

A desire to know the Lord will put together all the pieces of the puzzle and provide you with the answers you seek. Ask God to reveal the truth to you and He will. After all, there is only one true, living God, and He has given us all access to go to Him directly. That's all I did: I asked and I prayed, and surely He is revealing all things to me. If you know the Lord, spend time with him and see your world change before your eyes.

The changes in your life will be apparent to you and to others. As Shelley states in her testimony, the pieces of the puzzle that is called life will begin to fit together perfectly.

God is love, so in His presence you will experience that love and want to share it with others. Even when others hate you, you will come to a place where you can see the consequences of their actions, be moved with compassion, and have only love for them and a hope that they will see where they are going wrong. You will begin to pray for them, and the anger in you will subside and be replaced with peace.

God is peace, so when you are in His presence, that peace will wash over you. You will go through the most challenging times in your life and you will not be defeated. It may be that your home or car is being re-possessed, you may be facing a prison sentence, your nearest and dearest may be turning on you, your marriage or relationship may be breaking down...and through it all, you will have a peace you have never known. You will trust the Lord to the extent that you let Him take the reins in your life.

Praying to God will reap rewards!

ACTIVITY 10

What is prayer? ....

....

Where in the Bible will you find the prayer template? ....

How often should you pray? ....

....

What is the purpose of praying? ....

....

....

How often do you pray? ....

....

What happens when you pray? ....

....

List three types of prayer: ....

....

....

Notes: ....

CHAPTER 11
THE ESSENCE OF FASTING

Fasting is an essential part of the Christian life and is, more often than not, mentioned with prayer. Think of them as partners, prayer and fasting. Immediately after Jesus was baptised, He was led up into the wilderness by the Holy Spirit where He fasted for forty days and nights:

"Then Jesus was led up by the Spirit into the wilderness to be tempted by the devil. And when He had fasted forty days and forty nights, afterward He was hungry."

[Matthew 4:1-2 NKJV]

Moses also fasted for forty days and nights when he was in the presence of God to receive the tablets with the Ten Commandments. This tells us undeniably that fasting is important for every Christian. I'm not saying you have to fast for forty days and nights—you are not here to save the world, so just keep it simple!

When we fast, we bring our flesh man under submission and strengthen the spirit man. Fasting disciplines our minds and bodies and allows the Holy Spirit to work with our spirit. It is a sign of humility and surrender to God and a desire to be closer to Him. Fasting and prayer yields the Fruit of the Spirit in us and strengthens us. It is empowering to the individual.

So why did Jesus fast? Jesus had to keep His human side under subjection and remain extremely close to His Father. The fact that He came to us as flesh and blood means that He experienced the same things we do: hunger, exhaustion, pain, hurt, anger. He cried and, above all, He loved—loved US. His flesh would have battled against His spirit in much the same way as it does in us. Jesus knew what He had to go through, so the forty days and nights of fasting at the start of His ministry was to strengthen and empower Him; to discipline the flesh, strengthen the spirit and prepare Him for the task ahead.

Jesus' flesh man and logical mind would have reasoned and fought against submitting to the brutality of a people who hated Him for no reason. He would have spent that period of fasting in the presence of God, praying to and being strengthened and encouraged by His Father. He had to overcome the temptations of the devil, which He did and came out victorious.

Jesus fasted and resisted the devil's temptations even though He hadn't eaten for so long. He never gave in to temptation from the enemy. There have been many debates as to whether or not Jesus drank water during this time, with some claiming it is impossible for a human to go this length of time without water. Remember, with man these things are not possible, but with God, *all* things are possible [Matthew 19:26].

The strength of their argument lies in the sentence that states, "afterward He was hungry", with no mention of Him being thirsty. To understand this a little better we need to follow the scriptures back to the time when Moses fasted for forty days and nights. Moses neither ate nor drank for the forty days and nights when He was in God's presence.

"Moses was there with the Lord forty days and forty nights; he ate no bread and drank no water."

[Exodus 34:28 NKJV]

Moses was in the presence of God and Jesus is God! Moses is not greater than Jesus, so I say no, Jesus did not drink during His forty days and nights of fasting, because not only is He greater than Moses, but He had such a greater purpose that there is no comparison. Moses led approximately one million people out of slavery, but Jesus saved the world—billions and billions of people since the beginning of time. Is there really a comparison here?

Even today, if God chooses a mere human being to spend forty days and nights in His presence fasting without food or drink, like Moses, he will do it, because all things are possible in Him if we believe.

Jesus teaches us what to do and what not to do when we fast. There should always be a purpose to your fasting. Never fast to please others, don't make a public declaration to impress people, and always do it with a willing heart or there is no point in doing it at all. The scribes and Pharisees made public spectacles of their fasting and Jesus did not like this. Only God needs to see our fasting. "And whenever you are fasting, do not look gloomy like the hypocrites, for they put on a sad and dismal face [like actors, discolouring their faces with ashes or dirt] so that their fasting may be seen by men. I assure you and most solemnly say to you, they [already] have their reward in full. But when you fast, put oil on your head [as you normally would to groom your hair] and wash your face so that your fasting will not be noticed by people, but by your Father who is in secret; and your Father who sees [what is done] in secret will reward you."

[Matthew 6:16-18 AMP]

When you dedicate time to fasting and prayer and willingly allow the Lord to cleanse, strengthen and empower you, He will reward you openly. This means that others will see you growing spiritually and your calling will be apparent to all, so you do not need to try to control this or speed past the Lord. There will be many reasons why you fast throughout your Christian life and there are many examples in the Bible of men and women fasting for specific purposes.

King David committed adultery with Uriah's wife, who became pregnant [2 Samuel 12]. Uriah was a soldier in David's army, so David tried to cover up his actions by giving instructions for Uriah to be placed at the front of the battlefield to be killed, and he was. This sin greatly grieved God because David had taken an innocent life to hide his wrongdoing, and there were consequences for his actions.

David fasted to save the life of his son who was born out of this sin, and the duration depended on the evidence of whether his son lived or died. It is worth noting the great faith David had in God. He trusted God to do what was right, even though he did not get the outcome he asked for. He never blamed God for his own wrongdoings and accepted the consequences of his actions. After David's child died, and he realised he had not received what he'd asked for, he got up, washed, changed his clothes and went to worship the Lord before he ate. That is the kind of unshakeable faith and obedience we need to have before God. David did not deflect or justify his actions, nor did he blame God or try to reason his way out of the situation.

Fasting empowers the Christian to do amazing things. We are told that a man brought his son who was possessed by a demonic spirit to Jesus' disciples for them to cast out the demon, but they were not able to [Mark 9:17-18].

Only Jesus could cast out the demon because evil cannot remain in His presence. The disciples tried but were unsuccessful, and when they asked Jesus why they were not able to cast out the spirit, Jesus said:

"This kind can come out by nothing but prayer and fasting."

[Mark 9:29 NKJV]

So we have confirmation from Jesus that we must fast and pray to enable us to deal with such circumstances. Fasting empowers us to do the things Jesus did. It should be a priority in the life of a Christian, but many new converts find it confusing and are not sure what type of fast to engage in. They often fast because they are told to do so, without having the full understanding as to why they are doing it and what the benefits are.

Fasting because you are told to do so and abstaining from certain foods may make you feel physically refreshed, but what did you really achieve with it?

Daniel's Fast

The following study of the prophet Daniel when he fasted for the Jewish people encompasses the real essence of fasting, together with prayer, to provide the new convert with a top-level understanding of what happens when we set our hearts to seek the Lord. Many churches engage in what is known as the 'Daniel Fast', or the 21-Day Fast. This fast is structured around the prophet Daniel when he fasted for twenty-one days [Daniel:10], but, as always, there is much confusion and misunderstanding where this fast is concerned, leaving many new Christians feeling confused throughout the process.

This is the current version of the Daniel Fast used in many churches today:

- The church comes together in a time of fasting and prayer
- A specified duration of twenty-one days is agreed in advance
- Christians are instructed not to eat meat [sometimes fish] for the duration of the fast
- They are instructed to fast from when they wake up, or a specified time, and to finish at a specified time each day
- They are instructed to ask God for a set of predetermined things

There is nothing wrong with bringing the church together in fasting and prayer—it is a good thing—but with this type of fast the spiritual meaning is often lost as many don't fully understand why they are doing it, why it has to be for twenty-one days and why they can't eat meat. These are just some of the questions which remain unanswered to many seeking a greater understanding.

To understand this type of fast we will look at the following points about the actual fast which Daniel undertook:

- What Daniel was fasting and praying for   Purpose
- Why Daniel fasted for twenty-one days   Duration
- Why Daniel ate no meat and only drank water   Abstinence
- How long Daniel waited for the answer   Patience
- The answer Daniel received from God   Result

The Background

The Jewish people had been taken into captivity by King Nebuchadnezzar when Daniel was a young man [Book of Daniel]. He and three other young men were employed in the palace to work for the king. Daniel led a disciplined life of prayer and fasting and constantly sought God for answers regarding the life of God's people. Through God, Daniel was given many visions of the future, some of which are still being fulfilled today, and was also able to interpret other people's dreams and visions. While fasting, Daniel mourned for three weeks—not the mourning of a personal death or bereavement, but a sad cry to God in fasting and prayer on behalf of the Jewish people.

"In those days I, Daniel, had been mourning for three entire weeks. I ate no tasty food, nor did any meat or wine enter my mouth; and I did not anoint [refresh, groom] myself at all for the full three weeks."

[Daniel 10:2-3 KJV]

This type of prayer is intercessory, as Daniel was praying not for himself but was 'interceding' or going to God in prayer for someone else—a whole nation, in fact. Daniel was praying to know what the plight of the Jewish people would be. He was not praying for vain, prideful things; he was not praying for the new car or the riches of the world. His prayer was holy in God's eyes.

But why three weeks? We learn from the angel who brought the message to Daniel that his prayer was actually answered from the first day he started fasting, but the messenger angel had been delayed by twenty-one days.

Daniel did not plan to fast for twenty-one days, because he would not have known that the messenger angel was fighting in the heavenly atmosphere for that period of time. He planned to fast and seek the Lord for an answer and was willing to keep going until he received it. He did not stop after seven days, or ten days, or twenty days. He stopped when he received a concrete answer to his prayer and this was on the twenty-first day.

Now to the matter of why Daniel ate no pleasant food or meat, nor drank wine. When Daniel and the other young men were brought into the palace to be trained and educated to serve the king, the king gave instructions for them to be fed well with the same delicacies and wine that he himself drank.

"The king assigned a daily ration for them from his finest food and from the wine which he drank. They were to be educated and nourished this way for three years so that at the end of that time they were [prepared] to enter the king's service."

[Daniel 1:5 AMP]

However, this troubled Daniel because the king and this nation worshipped idols and false gods and ate foods that the Jewish people were prohibited from eating by the Law given to Moses.

"But Daniel made up his mind that he would not defile [taint, dishonour] himself with the king's finest food or with the wine which the king drank; so he asked the commander of the officials that he might [be excused so that he would] not defile himself."

[Daniel 1:8 AMP]

And in verse 12 he convinced the commander of the officials:

"Please, test your servants for ten days, and let us be given some vegetables to eat and water to drink."

They were forbidden from eating certain types of animals and other foods and they were certainly not supposed to eat anything offered up to idols or false gods. God knew the challenges that Daniel faced, so He worked in the background to bring Daniel into good standing with the chief of the palace officials, who oversaw the welfare of the young men.

Daniel asked if they could be fed with vegetables and water and not the king's delicacies, so from the outset Daniel refused to enjoy the spoils of palace life. The chief of the palace officials told Daniel he was afraid for his head if the king saw that they were losing weight and looking worse than the other young men. Daniel challenged him to test them for ten days and, sure enough, at the end of the ten days they looked healthier than the men who feasted on delicacies fit for a king.

Eating vegetables and drinking water was a lifelong sacrifice and commitment that Daniel made to the Lord, not just for the fast, and the Lord blessed him and the other young men by keeping them fit and healthy. The king's food that Daniel was offered went against his belief and would have compromised his faith, and he refused to do this.

Daniel fasted and prayed, patiently waiting for an answer from God. Finally, he received an answer. He was walking by the side of the River Tigris on the twenty-first day of his fast when an angel of the Lord appeared to him with an answer from God. Everyone who was with him ran off, terrified.

As new Christians you will get impatient sometimes, thinking God has not heard you and is not going to answer you, but you must ask the Lord to give you a good measure of faith and patience and believe that He will answer you. Eager and persistent prayer reaps great rewards and is advantageous to the person who is praying.

If we are to follow in Daniel's footsteps and fast like him, I would say that to decide to fast for twenty-one days from the outset changes the real spiritual meaning of the fast and weakens the faith element in it; we should not put a limit on the fast duration, but keep going until we get an answer, as Daniel did. This would show real faith in the Lord, to trust and believe that He will answer us.

If we were challenged with such a task, how many of us would immediately think, 'What if God doesn't answer me? I might be fasting for months'? If those are your first thoughts, you're probably not ready for the 'Daniel Fast'. Don't throw yourself into long, unmanageable fasts. Be guided and be wise. Remember, don't try to climb the mountain from the top, start at the bottom!

When you fast, don't worry about set fasts that you read about on the internet or try to follow fasts that come 'highly recommended'. You are the only person who will truly know what you have need of: spiritual strength and cleansing, the breaking of bad habits, greater faith, the strength to love those who are hurting you—the possibilities are endless. Be led by the Holy Spirit and not by 'man'.

NOWHERE LIKE IT

Holy fasting and prayer take you into the Holy of Holies, God's inner court: the most holy place, which is in God's presence. This is not a physical place but a spiritual place! There is nowhere else I'd rather be!

In a Nutshell:
- Fasting is a must for all Christians to strengthen our relationship with God. It brings us closer to God; it is our ultimate 'me time' with Him
- Fasting should be God-led and not man-led
- There must always be a purpose for your fast and this should not be fleshy, worldly or to ask for material things
- Fasting brings the flesh under subjection, so it is a time to discipline the flesh
- Fasting must be done willingly from the heart and not be forced upon you
- Fasting must never be a public show
- Fasting empowers you
- Don't fast for vain reasons, such as to lose weight or as part

of your calorie-controlled diet. You won't lose weight when you fast

- Time dedicated to fasting should include prayer, reading the Bible and worship
- Don't get caught up with the Daniel Fast or Esther's Fast or King David's fast. Use wisdom
- Your time with the Lord will be fruitful and He will lead you into which fast you need to do for specific purposes, such as whether you will need to do a full fast, where you neither eat nor drink; whether you need to fast around the clock; whether you should do a partial fast, which is to eat only at certain specified times; what types of foods to eat or drink during this period; and the duration of your fast.

Fasting Plan

When you feel ready and led to start your fasting journey, here is a simple three-day fasting plan for a new Christian. You can customise it to suit your purpose.

What to do	When to do it	How to do it
Fast	After your last meal of the day try not to eat until you end your fast the following day. Fast from when you wake up until lunch or longer if you wish. You can drink but not eat. Break your fast with a light meal. Don't be tempted to devour a huge meal directly after a fast; you will feel uncomfortable.	Say a prayer before you start your fast, dedicating the time to the Lord and telling Him why you are fasting. Decide on a time to break your fast, maybe at lunch or in the evening. During your fast, pray, read the scriptures, praise and spend some real quality time with the Lord.

Read the Scriptures	Find some time each day to read and meditate on the scriptures. Don't try to read too much at once; read only as much as you can take in and meditate on. Don't forget to say a simple prayer beforehand for revelation and understanding of the scriptures.	Recommended scriptures: Psalm 23 Psalm 27 Psalm 91 2 Corinthians 10
Pray	Set your alarm fifteen minutes earlier than usual and have some 'me time' with the Lord before the hustle and bustle of the day begins. Put some time aside at the end of the day as well. Make your personal time with the Lord a priority.	Say a simple prayer to start your day. Let your prayers be pertinent to the purpose of the fast. Tell the Lord everything; don't hold back. You can pray at any time throughout the day. Also say a simple prayer of thanks-giving when you finish your fast each day.

If you are fasting and praying and believe that the Lord is not answering your prayers, you need to talk to Him about it. You must also be willing to wait patiently on the Lord. This, however, is easier said than done. So, what does it mean to wait on the Lord? We will look at this in the next chapter.

Recommended Reading

Daniel Chapter 10   Daniel Fasts
Matthew Chapter 6   Prayer and Fasting

ACTIVITY 11

Fasting is often partnered with what? ....

Fasting should be man-led! True or false?...

Why did Daniel fast for twenty-one days? ....

....

....

....

Why should the Christian fast?..

....

....

When I fast, I can lose weight. True or false? ....

Why did Jesus fast for forty days and nights? ....

....

....

How many people should you boast to when fasting and why? ....

....

Notes: ....

CHAPTER 12
WAITING ON THE LORD

What is really meant by waiting on the Lord? Are we waiting *on* the Lord or waiting *for* the Lord? The two terms, though used interchangeably, have very different meanings. As a race, humans are very impatient. We can be spoilt and demanding. But just as parents should teach and guide their child, the Lord teaches and guides us. Throwing a tantrum, kicking and screaming at the Lord, doesn't work. Trying to force Him to bow down to you doesn't work. Slandering Him and declaring that He hasn't given you what you want doesn't work. Love, patience and temperance are all characteristics of God and the godly person. That works!

To understand whether we are waiting on or for the Lord we must first address the concept of God's time and our time. God exists outside of time and space as we know it. Our time ticks by slowly, while God's is at a speed that we cannot comprehend. The following scripture gives us some idea of how God's timing transcends ours and why. If we are waiting for an answer for a few years, it seems like a lifetime to us, when in actual fact it is but a few seconds to God.

"Nevertheless, do not let this one fact escape your notice, beloved, that with the Lord one day is like a thousand years, and a thousand years is like one day."

[2 Peter 3:8 AMP]

So our time and God's time are literally worlds apart. The table below gives a rough calculation of the difference between our time and God's time and does not take into consideration leap years or any other calendar anomalies.

GOD HOURS	MAN YEARS
24	1000
12	500
6	250
3	125
1.5	62.5
1 HR	**41.66667 YRS**
[1 minute]	[253.47 days]

With these rough calculations, you can work out for yourself the equivalent of five or ten of our years in God's time. We are a demanding generation and as Christians we can get very impatient when we ask God for something. For some, a few months or years is too long to wait for an answer and they get frustrated, while others give up. Working on this premise, Jesus left us approximately two thousand years ago and to us that is a very long time, but in God's time it was approximately two days ago.

Now on to the subject of waiting... Are we waiting for someone or are we waiting on someone? To wait on (or, in older versions of the Bible, to wait upon) is to be in close proximity to the person. You are usually performing a task and serving or supporting the person in some way. The best example for this is a waiter/waitress serving customers: they are in close proximity when providing the service, then clean and dress the table for the next customers.

To wait for, however, is to not be in close proximity to the person or thing you are waiting for. A good example of this is to wait for a bus or for someone who is giving you a lift. You wait patiently with anticipation and expectation.

So when you have prayed to the Lord for something and are waiting for an answer, are you waiting upon the Lord (serving him), or are you waiting for Him to do something for you?

Many come to the Lord with their own agenda and a set of demands. They expect to receive but never to give! When you come to the Lord, don't worry about your demands, what you want and when you think you should get it; that mindset is all wrong.

"But first and most importantly seek [aim at, strive after] His kingdom and His righteousness [His way of doing and being right—the attitude and character of God], and all these things will be given to you also."

[Matthew 6:33 AMP]

Seek Him with all your heart and don't worry about your list of demands and your timescales. He knows why He called you and will provide you with everything you will need for the journey. Coming to the Lord and telling Him you want to be a professional footballer, or an actor, or expecting never to struggle, financially or otherwise, is a false reality that you have created for yourself. Seek to know what God's perfect will for your life is. What if He didn't create you for the purpose you crave? Does it mean that He has failed you? Absolutely not—it means you were determined to have your own way and as a Father, He said 'No!'

Even when we understand this concept and decide to wait for the Lord to do something for us, we can still become impatient and often not really sure what we should be doing during this time. Should we slip back into our old ways of partying, not bothering to worship with other church members and stopping praying or fasting? Most definitely not, quite the opposite! This is the time to wait upon the Lord.

This is the time to seek the Lord continuously by praying and fasting, believing in Him to take you through any struggles you are faced with, and reading and studying the Bible with a passion. It is this time of seeking and searching that confirms to the Lord that you really want to be with Him. It is a time in which you should connect with your personal praise and worship and put all your needs before the Lord, always remembering that He will do what is right for you. This is when you are in His presence (close proximity) and giving to Him rather than waiting for Him to give to you. During this time of waiting upon the Lord you are still receiving from Him, but you may not realise it. The Lord will use this precious time to bless and strengthen you:

"But they that wait upon the LORD shall renew their strength; they shall mount up with wings as eagles; they shall run, and not be weary; and they shall walk, and not faint."

[Isaiah 40:31 KJV]

The King James Version of the Bible says 'to wait upon', the New King James Version says 'to wait on' and newer versions, such as the Amplified, say 'to wait for'. True meanings of scripture often get lost with newer versions of the Bible, but we are all responsible for finding the true meanings through our relationship with God.

When waiting upon the Lord, it's easy to think it's quiet, and nothing is happening, but that's when everything is happening—but you can't see or understand it until it hits. Remember, Daniel was praying and waiting on the Lord with continuous prayer, not knowing that the messenger angel was fighting with top-level demons over Persia, which prolonged his journey and the answer. Then look at what happened when Daniel received his answer: the angel appeared to him and explained what had happened.

Know that God hears you and will answer you, but that you must learn to wait on Him to receive your blessings. While you are waiting for Him to do something for you, you need to wait on Him. Below are two examples of men of God who waited on the Lord and waited for the Lord.

David Waiting on the Lord

Many will know the story of David and Goliath, but there was so much more to David than killing Goliath. You can read all about David in the books of 1 & 2 Samuel in the Old Testament. David (meaning *beloved*) was a young shepherd and, at the age of seventeen, was anointed by the prophet Samuel to be king over all Israel. Immediately after the anointing he was sent back out with the sheep to keep watch over them, and life, it seemed, continued as normal. David was not ready to be king at that age and he could not have fathomed what God had in store for him. He could not see the bigger picture at that moment in his life, nor know that he would be the greatest earthly king that ever lived and a man after God's own heart.

David did not become king until thirteen years later, when he was thirty. But what did he do during that time? He did not wait for the Lord to make him king; he waited on the Lord! He tended the sheep daily, protected them from a lion by killing it with his bare hands, and praised and worshipped God with songs and music from his harp. He spent a lot of time with God, in His presence, praying and trusting in Him. No palace training, no delicacies from the king's table, no one waiting on him 'hand and foot'.

David started working for Saul (the then king of Israel) for a while and God began to do great things with David, so Saul became jealous and tried relentlessly to kill him. What was God doing with David? He was training David, in the background, away from the glare and criticism of people. David received practical training from real-life situations; however, not many Christians realise when God is training them. David went through many trials and tests, protecting the sheep, learning to obey God, being faithful to Him, running from Saul and even sparing Saul's life when he could easily have killed him. David knew God would not want him to do this, so he remained on the run from Saul until God was ready to bring him out of that situation—constantly running, hiding and living a less than dignified life.

David was called to be a king over all of Israel—God was to trust him to look after His precious people—so the training was tough. He learnt how to praise God through the pain and trials of life, such as when he was on the run from King Saul. David did not make any demands of God. Had he been waiting for God, he would not have been in God's presence. He learnt how to love Saul regardless of all the things Saul put him through; he learnt how to spend personal time with God and to listen to Him; and, most importantly, he learnt how to 'wait on the Lord'.

The greater the calling and the more work God has to do with you, the harder the training will be. Don't try to rush Him, because He refuses to give you tasks that you are not prepared for.

God *always* has so much more for us than we can imagine for ourselves.

There are times when Christians struggle in ministries they may not have been called to because, somehow, they have managed to bypass God's process and training. There are two reasons for this:

The first is *nepotism* in the church. Some leaders will put Christians into ministries they are not called to be in because they are a family member, a close friend or are deemed more worthy than others. Jesus does not like partiality and taught against it. This needs to stop. Those who engage in partiality are assisting in preventing that person from seeking their true calling and are undermining God's plan for that person's life. God will never hand things to us that we cannot handle. He will always let us go through the right processes so that we can deal with the challenges of that ministry.

The second reason is when a Christian chooses to bypass God's process to fulfil their own desires. They decide what they want and they are single-minded in achieving it.

In both cases you may very well lead a good life, but you will have missed out on a great life—that is, God's perfect will for you. You cannot be partial and choose what you consider to be the most desirable ministries in God's kingdom, because you will be going against His will and there are always consequences.

The opposite of that situation is to be called to a ministry by God but have members or leaders try to block your way because they do not deem you worthy. There is a short, decisive answer to this non-problem: don't pay it any mind! Show me the man or woman who is greater than God and I will say 'be afraid'. Until then, don't worry about the challenges, the character assassinations behind your back, the discouraging words into your spirit, the sideways glances; talk to God about it and trust Him to supernaturally move those little hills out of the way. They are not even mountains to God.

God will use the blockages to train you, strengthen you and open your eyes to the world you have been called into. He will remove them for you, break down the barriers and place you just where you should be. Don't worry about how or when, just know that no one can stop you but yourself.

"What then shall we say to all these things? If God is for us, who can be [successful] against us? He who did not spare [even] His own Son, but gave Him up for us all, how will He not also, along with Him, graciously give us all things? Who will bring any charge against God's elect [His chosen ones]? It is God who justifies us [declaring us blameless and putting us in a right relationship with Himself]."

[Romans 8:31-33 AMP]

If He can give up His own Son to save us, imagine what He will do to defend His people who have been saved!

The following is a short study about Zacchaeus, who sought out the Lord and waited patiently for Him. He did not know God and was not in His presence like David, but he had a desire to know Him and persevered until he succeeded. We too should be determined, strategic and patient like Zacchaeus.

Zacchaeus Waiting for the Lord
Who was he?
You can read all about Zacchaeus in the Gospel of Luke, Chapter 19, in the New Testament. Zacchaeus was determined to find Jesus and he did not stop until he found Him. He had many challenges along the way but never gave up. He positioned himself in the right place and waited for the Lord to come passing by.

What was happening in the natural world?
Zacchaeus was very rich. He'd heard about Jesus and set his heart on finding Him, but he was hindered by the great multitudes and by being a small man. His search for Jesus was certainly challenging for him. As he tried to get to Jesus there were many obstacles in his way, but these did not deter him. He eventually put a strategy in place to get away from the crowd and run ahead of them. He climbed up into a tree and waited for Jesus to pass by. When Jesus saw him and told him to come down, Zacchaeus joyfully met the Lord and gave Him an account of himself. The Lord accepted Zacchaeus and confirmed that He would go to his home with him.

What happened spiritually?
Zacchaeus didn't know what Jesus looked like, who He was or where to find Him, but he decided to search for Him. He was small like a child and there were obstacles in the way (the multitude represented the obstacles). In his search, he overcame those obstacles, learnt what he was dealing with and became strategic. Everyone who comes to

the Lord is reborn a spiritual babe in Christ and will be faced with many challenges like Zacchaeus was.

When he found Jesus, Zacchaeus positioned himself to ensure that the Lord would not pass him by or leave him behind. His desire was great. Then Zacchaeus was patient and waited; he waited for the Lord to come to him. The Lord came to the place where Zacchaeus was waiting and looked up. Zacchaeus was in the right place—on high ground, or good ground.

The Lord answered Zacchaeus and told him that He would abide with him. This is what happens when we come to Jesus: he comes into our hearts and abides with us.

Zacchaeus experienced real joy in himself when he met the Lord. He confessed himself to the Lord and publicly showed his love for Him by making changes in his life, and we should do the same.

The Lord then told Zacchaeus what to do, and what He would do for Zacchaeus to achieve salvation—this is true conversion! Salvation is for everyone regardless of wealth, job, size, creed, colour, where you live or what you've done. The Lord is seeking those who have a desire to find Him and search for Him with all their hearts. Jesus came for the sinner, to abide and live within them through the Holy Spirit.

Recommended Reading

1 Samuel Chapter 16	David is Anointed to be King
Luke Chapter 19	Jesus Saves Zacchaeus

ACTIVITY 12

What is the difference between waiting on the Lord and waiting for the Lord?...

....

....

....

How did David wait? ....

....

Why did Zacchaeus climb up a tree? ....

....

....

How is God's time different from ours?...

....

Why did Saul try to kill David?...

....

....

Notes: ....

....

Seek God

I came upon a bird, more beautiful and perfect than ever I'd seen,
Who tried to fly away to pastures green.
He fought and struggled and wore himself down,
And wondered why he couldn't get off the ground.
He gazed at the other birds, and praised them for their beauty and
grace,
Then completely excluded himself from the race.

His mind confused, he sought to hide,
While searching for answers far and wide.
I came upon him again one day
And felt his pain as he walked my way.
"Little bird," I said, "why walk when you have wings?
"Birds were made to fly and sing,
"It is a most unnatural thing you do.
This is not the life for you."

I sat him down and asked him to sing.
He spoke and said, "I seem to fail at everything.
"I cannot fly, no matter how hard I try."
"Little bird," I said, "you are a clever thing,
"But even you cannot fly with a broken wing.
"You must seek and you will find
"The answers await you in front, not behind.
"So fly, little bird, fly."

He continued to look downhearted.
"My heart is so heavy," he said, "I don't know what to do."
"To love someone else," I replied, "you must, first, love you.
"Little bird with the broken wing,
"Divine loves come from within.
"Love God first, and all things will be revealed,
"Then slowly, but surely, your wing will be healed."

CHAPTER 13
THE DEFAULT POSITION

"For just as through one man's disobedience [his failure to hear, his carelessness] the many were made sinners, so through the obedience of the one Man the many will be made righteous and acceptable to God and brought into right standing with Him."

Romans 5:19 AMP

On the day that Adam and Eve ate the fruit of the tree of knowledge of good and evil, they inherited the knowledge and all that it had to offer. They lost the will to do the right thing and this became inherent in mankind. They had the knowledge but had not gained it through experience. The curse of sin (not individual sin, but the sin of the world) was that we, 'mankind', gave away our birthright and the right to all that God had for us.

Our birthright was to have dominion over all the Earth and the life in it from a position of holiness and authority, because we knew no sin. Holiness was our default position. When we gave up our birthright to that holiness, we also turned the natural order upside down, not just for humans but for the world and all other life in it. It was no longer a perfect world. An imperfect ruler cannot rule over a perfect world; eventually the ruler will corrupt it. So our default position is now a sinful one in a fallen world, and no longer holiness in a perfect world. For this reason, Jesus had to come to give us our birthright back.

Our peaceful, beautiful world became beset with disasters, one after another. Jesus did not come to fix this world or to patch us up to continue living in it; He came to make all things new, a new people and a new world.

"And He who sits on the throne said, 'Behold, I am making all things new.'"

[Revelation 21:5 AMP]

In this world as we know it, there are only two forces, the force of 'good' (God) and the force of 'evil' (Satan). When Adam and Eve gave away our birthright, we did not have a choice in the matter, but now we do have a choice through Jesus. We can choose to be with God or to be with Satan. In choosing one, the other will be rejected, and most people find this easy enough to understand.

However, if you do not make a choice, you are in the default position, which is sin, or Satan's domain, and there is no middle ground or grey area. If you do not choose God, by default you have chosen Satan, because you will remain in your sin.

The default position is inherited—we are all born in it—so we must make a conscious decision to get out of it. This is the choice Jesus gave back to us. As stated earlier, the human race came under the sin nature when mankind fell, and it is the worst position we could be in, which is why God gave us a way out. Many, however, do not realise that they are in the default position, so they do not think they have to make a choice to get out of it. The only way to God the Father is through Jesus the Son.

"Jesus said unto him [his disciple Thomas], I am the way, the truth, and the life: no man comes unto the Father, but by me."

[John 14:6 KJV]

There is no other way to get to the Father. No matter how much we challenge this, criticise it and reason against it, it is what it is. Christian teachings that sidestep Jesus will not help you on your Christian journey. All those who profess to know God but do not know Jesus will not find their way back to Him without his Son! You know by now that to accept Jesus, you make a decision in your heart and follow through with a public declaration. In short, you make a choice. You also know by now that *not* choosing Jesus is detrimental to your very existence; so why do people refuse to choose Jesus, even though it can only be a good thing for them?

Often in life you will hear people say, 'I'm a good person, so I should go to heaven' or, 'I've never harmed anyone, so are you saying I will go to hell?' or, 'How can God say He loves me and then send me to hell? I would never do this to someone I love.' Obviously, there are good non-Christians in this world who have caring hearts and who do a lot for others and there is no disputing this. However, no amount of good deeds and works can pay your way into heaven. You do not qualify by your efforts, your abilities, or how much time and money you put into doing things for others. If this was the case, salvation would have a price. Some would qualify and others wouldn't due to different ability levels, different amounts of wealth, different moral standings and so on. Salvation would become elitist, exclusive and highly competitive, and many of us would be excluded. Then we would declare that it wasn't fair and become resentful, giving rise to a whole different set of complaints.

God devised a plan to allow His only Son to die to save us. Do you think this was an easy thing to do? Do you think God enjoyed seeing His Son being brutalised and ultimately killed by those who committed this sin in the first place? If we decide not to choose Him because we can't be bothered to live righteous lives, we should not blame God. He didn't do this to us and He is not sending anyone to hell. Hell was created for the devil and his followers, not for you or me.

Instead, God has given us a more perfect way to receive salvation. It takes no physical effort or special ability, there is no competition to win or lose, we don't have to be rich to afford it and we don't have to work for it or make any sacrifices. We just have to say 'yes' to Jesus and ask Him to save us. It cannot be any simpler than that.

Everyone has the same chance of receiving salvation; how much more can God possibly do for us? If you choose to reject Jesus, or do not make a choice at all and continue living your life as dictated by yourself, no matter how good a person you think you are, you remain in the default position and salvation will not be yours. When you die you will not go into the presence of God; you will go to a terrible place to await the final judgement.

The Bible tells us about two people who died. One, a beggar, dies in Christ and the other, a rich man, dies without Christ. We get a glimpse of what happens after death for those who choose God and those who remain in the default position or choose Satan.

"Now it happened that the poor man died and his spirit was carried away by the angels to Abraham's bosom [paradise]; and the rich man also died and was buried. In Hades [the realm of the dead], being in torment, he looked up and saw Abraham far away and Lazarus in his bosom. And he cried out, 'Father Abraham, have mercy on me, and send Lazarus so that he may dip the tip of his finger in water and cool my tongue, because I am in severe agony in this flame.' But Abraham said, 'Son, remember that in your lifetime you received your good things [all the comforts and delights], and Lazarus likewise bad things [all the discomforts and distresses]; but now he is comforted here [in paradise], while you are in severe agony.'"

[Luke 16:22-25 AMP]

There is a huge gulf between the two destinations. Those who die in Christ will be in peaceful bliss and the others will be tormented in a hot, miserable place.

There is a misguided belief that many live by, that they can be Christians in their own way, and the answer to that is, 'No, they can't.' Many believe they can love God in their hearts while never having fellowship with their fellow Christians, going to church or reading the Bible. They decide to do it their own way. Actually, you have to do it God's way—otherwise, you will find yourself in the default position, because you are not living Christ's way. Jesus provides a support network for us:

"And let us consider [thoughtfully] how we may encourage one another to love and to do good deeds, not forsaking our meeting together [as believers for worship and instruction], as is the habit of some, but encouraging one another; and all the more [faithfully] as you see the day [of Christ's return] approaching."

[Hebrews 10:24-25 AMP]

We must consider each other in love, support and encourage each other, and not abandon or neglect gathering to do good together. Refusing to worship together is not acceptable to the Lord. The Bible also states that we should do this a lot more often as the final day approaches. The day being referred to is the day when Jesus returns and those who chose Him will be taken up into heaven with Him. The days leading up to this day, which are the days we are in now, are referred to as 'the last days', and they are not good, as we can see. There is real suffering in the world, the enemy is attacking from all angles and we are plagued with natural disasters, so we need to support and strengthen each other.

FACT

Nowhere in the Bible does it state that you can do 'it' your way, whatever 'it' is. If you refuse to be in fellowship as Christians, worship and strengthen each other and allow yourself to be taught and guided by those called to lead, you are open to attacks from the enemy and will not have a support network around you.

If we were meant to be alone and have no interaction with others, but worship God on our own terms in the confines of our homes, Jesus would have taught this to His disciples, and it would have been written in the Bible.

Although the gospel is preached and taught on a global scale and many people have given their lives to ensure the Bible is available in many different languages, there is still a lot of resistance as many refuse to accept Jesus as Lord, or even acknowledge that there is a God or higher power who created us. There are many reasons for this; we could not possibly address them all in this book, and certainly not in-depth, but the following are just a few excuses that keep popping up in this society.

Blockages to Accepting Jesus

There are many reasons people reject Jesus and will not accept that there is a God. A few are mentioned here but there are many more. You will notice that most refer to the first person, 'I this' and 'I that'. As a people we tend to make everything about ourselves, and we see everything from our viewpoint. When we are not doing this, we like to deflect or shift the blame onto something or someone else, often onto the very person who is trying to help us.

People often don't like to look at themselves. They are afraid of facing their fears and dealing with them. It is easier to pretend we are one way when we are another. Correction and criticism, constructive or otherwise, is a big 'no'. Even those who profess that they can take constructive criticism rarely appreciate it when it is given. We live in a selfish world. If it's not what we want or how we want it, we are not interested; if we don't understand it, we reject or try to harm it; if we have been hurt, we are not prepared to move past it and allow ourselves to be healed. If you are looking for an excuse not to accept Jesus, you will find one—or the devil will certainly find one for you—and it will be very convincing!

<u>I don't want anyone to force their beliefs on me!</u>
No one can force you to accept Jesus as your Lord and Saviour. It cannot be done and should not be done. You have to accept salvation by your own free will. If God wanted to force you to love Him, He would do it all by Himself, but He doesn't, so no one else can. If you feel you are being pressured, be wary. Make sure you accept the Lord because you believe in Him and not because you believe in the person who is trying to convince you, no matter how charismatic they seem to be.

As a Christian, you should preach and teach the gospel. Be patient with the non-believer and do not get angry with them. Remember, you were once in that position, when you did not believe and thought you had all the answers, rejecting anyone who shared the faith with you. There is an urgency for us to preach the gospel today, but this is not to be confused with pressuring someone into submission.

The urgency lies in the fact that no one knows when it will be their time to leave this world: today, tomorrow, next month, next year—we have absolutely no idea. Jesus never forced anyone to follow Him. When Jesus sent His disciples to spread the gospel, He directed them by saying, 'if people do not receive you, move on.'
"And He said to them, take nothing for the journey, neither staffs nor bag nor bread nor money; and do not have two tunics apiece. Whatever house you enter, stay there, and from there depart. And whoever will not receive you, when you go out of that city, shake off the very dust from your feet as a testimony against them."

[Luke 9:3-5 NKJV]

The reason they were told to take nothing with them is because the Lord wanted them to depend solely on Him and to start building their faith in Him and not in their own abilities. The instruction to "shake the dust from [their] feet" means we should not argue or try to force anyone to accept the Word of God; we must move on to the next person without condemning them or taking it personally. You may preach to them today (sowing a seed) and the next year or a lifetime later they may give their heart to the Lord. The "testimony against them" means that heaven has logged this moment, when someone shared the gospel with them and they rejected it, so they will never have an excuse to say they didn't know anything about Him.

There are billions of people in the world who need to hear the gospel, so we must keep moving on to get to as many people as possible. It is not for us to labour at trying to change someone's mind; we must leave the Holy Spirit to work with people's hearts and draw them to the Lord. If someone hardens their heart and mind against the Lord, no amount of cajoling will change them.

I have to sort myself out first.

If we could sort ourselves out, we would not have need for a Saviour! You can stop doing whatever you are doing, buy a new outfit, polish up your car and look the part when you step into the church building, but God knows the mess you are in. Don't attempt to impress people; they can't help you. Just bring your weak, broken self to God and He will 'build you up' so much better than you were before you came to Him.

Because many people don't know or understand God's grace, they think they have to 'clean up', start living right, stop drinking or taking drugs, be presentable and impress when they start going to church. Nothing could be further from the truth; this is just another one of the enemy's lies. Jesus did not come to save perfect, righteous beings—there is no perfect human being.

Jesus ate and drank with the sinners and the tax collectors. He was criticised for this, and when He heard his critics challenging His disciples He responded:

"…'Those who are healthy have no need of a physician, but [only] those who are sick; I did not come to call the righteous, but sinners [who recognise their sin and humbly seek forgiveness].'"

[Mark 2:17 AMP]

When you are sick you go see the doctor to make you better; you don't heal yourself, then go to the doctor. What would be the point? As I said, if we were perfect or holy, we would have no need for a Saviour. Trying to 'fix up' before you ask God for help is futile. If you were 'all together' you wouldn't need Him. Stop trying to do it by yourself and ask for His help. Jesus came to save the sinner, the broken, the outcast, the sick and the poor—not the perfect, because we are not perfect!

<u>I'd have to make too many sacrifices.</u>
You make more sacrifices when you are in the world than when you are in Christ. To remain in the world is to make the ultimate sacrifice, and that is to give up your soul, your eternal life. In the Old Testament, long before the birth of Jesus, many sacrifices were required to atone (compensate, make amends) for sin. Many ceremonial laws, festivals and burnt offerings were practised.

Today, because of Jesus, we are no longer required to make any such sacrifices. If we try to atone for sins by continuing with these practices, we are saying that what Jesus did was not enough, and we know better so we are doing better. The Lord is not putting us under any such pressure; all He asks for is our 'sacrifice of praise' and to live holy lives in Him. Is that really a sacrifice? Are you receiving such great rewards from this life that you are not interested in what the Lord has for you?

"Through Him, therefore, let us at all times offer up to God a sacrifice of praise, which is the fruit of lips that thankfully acknowledge and confess and glorify His name."

[Hebrews 13:15 AMP]

God is asking us to praise Him, give thanks to Him and be like Him, living a life of love. We are not required to eat certain foods, wear specific clothing or accessories, or uphold any religious festivals. There are no set times or durations for studying the Bible, fasting or praying. How much easier can God make it for us to choose Him?

<u>I won't be able to enjoy my life if I become a Christian now.</u>
Christians enjoy life. We live, we love, we marry, we travel, we eat and drink, we wear lovely clothes and we laugh (a lot). We enjoy our lives in Christ.

I'm not ready to make that kind of commitment.

As stated earlier, if you want to find a reason not to make a commitment to the Lord, you will find one or the enemy will find one for you. You've tried everything else, so why not try Jesus? God wants to give us so much, so if nothing else you should at the very least be curious.

"'For I know the plans and thoughts that I have for you,' says the Lord. 'Plans for peace and well-being and not for disaster, to give you a future and a hope.'"

[Jeremiah 29:11 AMP]

God has plans for your life. People make all kinds of commitments throughout their lives, but struggle to commit to the Lord. They are not ready; the commitment is too great; they won't have any more fun. We act as though we are doing the Lord a favour and He should wait until we are good and ready. Even more alarmingly, we act as if we have all the time in the world.

But time is not your friend; it waits for no one! It does not slow down to accommodate you, nor does it come around again to give you a second chance. Time was set by God and it keeps going; it does not answer to you. It steals away your youth, beauty and opportunity. In short, it does not belong to you and you cannot control it. No one knows how much time has been allotted to them in this world, so when the Lord says, 'If you want me, I am here; if you need me, I am here; I will give you more than you can ever imagine', why do we respond with, 'I'm not ready to make that kind of commitment'?

I couldn't look the way I want.

The way Christians dress or look has been a topic of much discussion, debate and preaching through the ages. The Bible does not say you should not take care of your appearance or that you cannot wear jewellery or colour and style your hair. The outward appearance should be the least of our worries. It is the beauty of the inner heart that God loves.

"Your adornment must not be merely external—with interweaving and elaborate knotting of the hair, and wearing gold jewellery, or [being superficially preoccupied with] dressing in expensive clothes;

but let it be [the inner beauty of] the hidden person of the heart, with the imperishable quality and unfading charm of a gentle and peaceful spirit, [one that is calm and self-controlled, not overanxious, but serene and spiritually mature] which is very precious in the sight of God."

[1 Peter 3:3-4 AMP]

When you come to the Lord, just come as you are and don't worry about what you look like. It is your heart and your desire to follow Him that He is concerned with. If your dress sense is a little risqué, the Holy Spirit will work with you (if you let Him) to assess yourself as you progress, and you will be able to decide what to keep and what to shake off.

Christians all over the world do not dress the same. You have the casual dresser, the smart dresser, the 'I'm-on-the-red-carpet dresser', and the cultural dresser. The Lord will not take away your creativity or your desire to adorn yourself. He just asks that you keep it in moderation and concentrate more on your heart than your outward appearance.

It is also worth noting that, if you come to the Lord with piercings or tattoos or anything else you adorned yourself with in the world, He will welcome you with open arms. Let Him work with you as no one else can.

Our world puts too much emphasis on outward appearance. Your looks do not define your heart or your love for the Lord, and no one should be able to convince you otherwise. Although God does not hold our past against us, if we try to bring that past into our future then that becomes a problem. Saying that, God is not interested in Christians 'looking the part'. The scribes and Pharisees in Jesus' time looked the part but were completely corrupt inside and harmful to the people they should have been protecting, and Jesus did not like it. He was angry with them for leading people astray and adding to their suffering.

"Woe to you, [self-righteous] scribes and Pharisees, hypocrites! For you are like whitewashed tombs which look beautiful on the outside, but inside are full of dead men's bones and everything unclean. So you, also, outwardly seem to be just and upright to men, but inwardly you are full of hypocrisy and lawlessness."

[Matthew 23:27-28 AMP]

They looked the part but their hearts were unclean, cold and without love—just like the bones of the dead, with no life in them. Jesus was not in their hearts and they were hypocrites. Don't use the way you look to hide an unrighteous lifestyle, because it cannot be hidden from God.

When God looks at you, He sees the blood of His Son Jesus Christ; then He looks into your heart to see if love is dwelling there. He does not see your latest designer shoes or your bright green hair or your tattoos. If, however, He looks into your heart and sees self-worship, pride, vanity, hatred or idolatry of the material things you own, that's when you need to be concerned. When you dress up your heart with love, forgiveness and tenderness, removing hate, greed and self-righteousness, then you are dressed well.

Christians are just a bunch of hypocrites.
No, Christians are not a bunch of hypocrites! While I am not disputing that there are hypocrites in the world, they are not a special breed of humans exclusive to Christianity. The word *hypocrite* originates from the Greek word 'hypokrites', which means 'stage actor, pretender, dissembler'. A hypocrite is a person who professes to be one way when in actual fact they are another way. In the case of a Christian, they may preach that people should have high morals and principles when they themselves are not living a high moralistic life and are not practising what they preach. Someone who condemns others for the same things they do in secret would be classed as a hypocrite.

On that premise, let's focus for a moment on some major institutions and establishments in the world: governments, politics, education, healthcare, family institutions, the world of the rich and famous—I could name every area of life and you will find loving, faithful, generous, true people and you will find damaged people, 'hypocrites' who don't really believe what they are publicly declaring.

How often is it revealed in the media that someone claiming to lead a healthy lifestyle has died suddenly from a drug overdose? Someone passes a new law whilst breaking it themselves, or someone professes to be looking after the vulnerable while abusing them.

Unfortunately, it is prevalent in the world today and not sacred to any one establishment. When a person becomes a Christian, they are not immediately made perfect. They strive to be like Christ, but it is a lifelong process.

Remember, Sanctification is the cleaning-up process where the Holy Spirit works with the new Christian from the beginning of their journey and throughout their life. The person still has free will and is able to make their own decisions. They can choose to hold on to the person they once were and refuse to let the Holy Spirit work with them to clean them up.

They are babes in Christ and have to learn to live and think differently. They have the enemy snapping at their heels and the residue of past desires and habits they are now fighting against. They are not yet fully re-generated and now face new challenges. As is the nature of a baby, they stumble, fail sometimes, fall, throw tantrums, wear themselves out and say and do the wrong things because they don't yet know any better. It is only through love and nurturing that the spiritual baby will grow into a mature spiritual adult. When we make mistakes, God forgives us, but man says, 'You are a hypocrite' or 'You are not a Christian'.

If we were perfect, we wouldn't need Jesus, so it is in our weakest moments that we experience His great strength. Don't let the world tell you that, because you are making some mistakes, you are a hypocrite. I'm not saying there are no hypocrites in the Christian faith, because they killed our Lord of Glory two thousand years ago and some would kill Him again now if they could, but let's keep it in context and not tarnish everyone with the same brush. God says that, when you fall, He will pick you up and you must hold onto that. As long as God forgives you, don't worry about what anyone else thinks of you. You are on the greatest journey of your life and you are striving for perfection, but are not yet perfect.

I don't really understand what it's all about.

You cannot be blamed for being more than a little confused by all the different denominations in the world, what is right or wrong, what to commit to and what to steer away from, who to believe or not to believe, and so on. The enemy has worked ceaselessly from the dawn of our creation to corrupt and destroy us. All this confusion in the world today comes directly from him influencing people to go against God's will.

If you want to find the truth, the first place to start searching is in your heart. Have a real desire to know the truth and ask God to help you find it. Whether you believe in Him or not at this point is of no consequence; simply set your heart on seeking the truth. Ask Him, 'Lord, are you real? Do you love me as much as people say you do? How can I find you? So many people say so many different things and I don't know what to believe. Please direct me to the right place or send someone to help me.'

The Lord will answer you. It won't be when you think He should or how you imagine He will, so be determined and keep asking. Think of all the things you did in life to find that perfect job or partner or home. Remember the level of commitment you showed until you achieved your goal.

People spend their entire lives searching, researching, conquering the highest mountain, sailing around the world or diving to the deepest depths of the ocean, all in the name of discovering life and living it. Apply the same principle when seeking the Lord. Don't ask once, then give up; if you desire an answer, don't stop until you get one. You will definitely get an answer from God, and I say that unreservedly.

"Then [with a deep longing] you will seek Me and require Me [as a vital necessity] and [you will] find Me when you search for Me with all your heart."

[Jeremiah 29:13 AMP]

Ask the Lord to lead you to the right person to help and guide you. Speak to a Christian with personal experience of Jesus Christ, not just a churchgoer or someone following a set of religious rules. Stay away from any newly founded sects, cults or religious groups claiming they have the answer to everything and are here to get you into heaven. No one can do that, only God. We are all responsible for finding the truth for ourselves by going directly to the Lord.

It's all a fantasy story; it's not real.
The truth is indeed fantastic but it is not a fantasy. It's very real. As Christians we are not here to prove God's existence or to prove that

Jesus is the Son of God or to prove that the Holy Spirit exists. Who can do this? We are here to spread the gospel through preaching and teaching, to share our experiences through our testimony, and to witness to others about the kingdom of God. People will either open their minds to give Jesus a chance or they won't, but it is entirely up to them. Every person who has died finally knows the truth – but by then it is too late. We will all know the truth one day, so what will you lose by asking the Lord to open your spiritual eyes and reveal it to you now while you can still do something about it?

Jesus was just a man, He's not the Son of God.
The Christian knows that Jesus is the Son of God. We know because our Holy Bible tells us, we know because God cannot lie, we know because He is real in our lives and we have real encounters and experiences with Him. We speak to Him and He speaks to us. Unless you are willing to step into His world and experience God for yourself, you will never really know and we cannot prove this to you. The journey is to be experienced.

I was a Christian once. I had some awful experiences with Christian people and I will never go into a church again!
The final chapter (Chapter 15) has been set aside just for you.

Recommended Reading

Romans Chapter 5	Death in Adam, Life in Christ
1 Corinthians Chapter 15	Our Hope in the Risen Christ

ACTIVITY 13

What is the Default Position? ....

....

What does God see when He looks at us?..

....

What prevented you from accepting Jesus? ....

....

What things are you holding onto in your heart? ....

....

....

....

How will I know Jesus is the Son of God?..

....

....

....

Notes: ....

....

CHAPTER 14
A LIFE MISUNDERSTOOD

Due to the many misconceptions about Christianity and the damage that innumerable religious practices cause, many people are absolutely terrified of stepping into a church. Many will come if family members or friends are already attending—some will push past the fear and enter—but others won't do it. As a Christian, it is very important to be Christlike and be actual imitators of Christ, not just on a Sunday or when you worship, but every day. Our actions can prevent others from coming to the Lord, and this should never be the case. Mistakes and struggles aside, we should never be a blockage to others finding Christ.

Many people continue to think they have to give up so much to follow Christ that they will not enjoy life anymore. You gain far more than what you give up. Let's just take a moment to look at some of the things the Lord will help us to give up when we commit to Him, in no particular order: substance abuse, lying, sexual promiscuity and deviances, stealing, harming yourself and others, committing murder, depression, living an unhappy life without hope—the list is endless. Why would you not want to give up these things? How do they enrich your life?

What is wrong with living a life that is good and healthy? A righteous life, giving and receiving respect and love? What is wrong with not abusing yourself or others and having a little dignity and self-worth? What is wrong with living to old age and not needlessly dying young?

Without quoting a lot of statistics, suicide is on the increase; depression and living without hope in a greater purpose has become the norm. People are putting their faith in their jobs, working to pensionable age and are barely able to enjoy the fruits of their labour when they retire, struggling with sickness and finally death. It's not a pretty picture and it's not a negative one; it is the reality of life. Do not mistake this world for a happy one. It is not a happy world that we live in, it's a fallen fragile world—so don't let anything or anyone stop you from seeking your happiness in God. Nothing else will stand the test of time.

If money were the answer, no rich person would ever take their life. They would all be happy and satisfied. If sexual relationships were the answer, there would be no separations once you find your partner. If taking substances could do it, we wouldn't need rehabilitation services. The answer is clearly not in the world. If you come to the Lord and your heart continues to yearn for worldly pleasures and you are not truly surrendered to Him, you are leaving yourself open to the same hopelessness that someone who is in the world and not in Christ experiences.

If you decide that you want to hold onto certain things, even when the Holy Spirit is telling you to let go, He won't force you to change. When you come to the Lord, you need to be willing to let Him change the 'old you' and clean you up, but if you resent the cleaning up in your heart and still desire the things of the world, there's nothing the Lord can do with you. Holding onto the things of the world while trying to hold onto the things of God is not possible: you will find yourself in the default position. You cannot straddle good and evil because one must win in the end.

One example of this situation can be seen in the history of Lot's wife in Genesis 19. Lot, the nephew of Abraham, went to live in a twinned city called Sodom and Gomorrah. The people of the city were wicked, evil and perverse. There was a great outcry against them, which the Lord heard and answered by sending two angels to destroy the city. Lot was a righteous man, actually the only righteous man living in the city, so the Lord told him to take his family and leave quickly before the angels destroyed the city.

"When they had brought them outside, one [of the angels] said, 'Escape for your life! Do not look behind you, or stop anywhere in the entire valley; escape to the mountains [of Moab], or you will be consumed and swept away.'"

[Genesis 19:17 AMP]

Lot and his family were instructed by the angels not to look back. This instruction is very symbolic in that it was not just the physical act of looking back that the Lord was advising against. He didn't want them to look back in their hearts, to miss the evil deeds of men or to yearn for them. The Lord showed mercy by saving them; however, Lot's wife did not really want to be saved, so she looked back and immediately became a pillar of salt.

"But Lot's wife, from behind him, [foolishly, longingly] looked [back toward Sodom in an act of disobedience], and she became a pillar of salt."

[Genesis 19:26 AMP]

When the consequence of doing something wrong is really bad, you know there is a greater spiritual meaning attached to it. In looking back, Lot's wife showed she was not happy with the mercy she and her family were being shown. She looked back with regret, refusing to move forward in life and embrace the new beginning the Lord had afforded them. She was already missing the pleasures and evils of the world she was being freed from. There was no love in her heart for the things of God, His mercy and His love. The Lord knew that she couldn't move on, so He wouldn't be able to work with her.

In much the same way, if we hold onto the world in our hearts and refuse to move forward with the Lord, He can't do much with us, and He will never force us to follow Him. Looking back limits our ability to move forward and hinders spiritual growth. What we gain in the Lord—love, joy, peace, self-respect and dignity, hope, self-worth and, did I mention, eternal life in the presence of God— far outweighs what we give up.

When the Holy Spirit works with you to clean you up, He doesn't throw you in a room, lock the door and leave you to sweat it out, to resurface drained, fragile and unsure of life. When He starts to dwell within you, He is so pure and holy that your cravings for things that are not holy or righteous will diminish over time, and the more you give of yourself to Him, the more He will remove those cravings. In some instances, when people are so hungry for the Lord, they can shake off old habits very quickly. Others, however, may take longer if they enjoy them so much that they don't want to fully let go. If this is the case, you will not be able to change or resist temptations through your own efforts. When you have a joy for the things of the Lord, you won't want to engage in the things of the world; you won't enjoy them anymore so you will want to give them up.

The Heart Condition

You have heard me mention many times that it is the heart the Lord works with, not the outward appearance or the things we are seen to be doing. The Heart Condition is everything to God. Everything we are and will be in God is based on His love for us and our love for Him and each other. He created us through love, He redeemed us through love and He has saved us through love.

It was because of that love that He gave us the greatest gift of all, Jesus Christ. It is very important for our hearts to be right. It doesn't matter what we do or how well we do it; if we have no love in our hearts, it's all for nothing.

"If I speak with the tongues of men and of angels, but have not love [for others growing out of God's love for me], then I have become only a noisy gong or a clanging cymbal [just an annoying distraction]. And if I have the gift of prophecy [and speak a new message from God to the people], and understand all mysteries, and [possess] all knowledge; and if I have all [sufficient] faith so that I can remove mountains, but do not have love [reaching out to others], I am nothing."

[1 Corinthians 13:1-2 AMP]

The love this scripture is referring to is not limited, erratic, inconsistent human love, with great emphasis on beauty, physical attraction and ego. It is the eternal, consistent, unchanging love of God. It is a love that does not see colour, does not define or judge a person by their physical attributes, does not change when that person causes them pain; it is a perfect love.

Many Christians, when they come to the Lord, get carried away with what they see, with the miracles, the preaching and teaching, and crave the 'power' of the Holy Spirit. They want to raise the dead, they want to preach to ten thousand, they want to prophesy and bring many souls to the Lord. While it is a good thing to have a desire for the Lord to use you, and work great things through you, nothing can or will work if you do not have love in your heart. Everything we do must be based on love for God and love for each other.

A great gift to pray for when you first come to the Lord to start building your faith on solid foundations is 'Crucifixion Love'. That love says, "Father, forgive them, for they know not what they do" (Luke 23:34 NKJV). Jesus' love was able to endure cruelty and allow him to pray for the same people who told lies about Him, spat in His face, pulled out His beard, stripped Him naked, beat and persecuted Him and finally killed Him. Pray for that love and, when it begins to show in you, everything you are destined to do will begin to flow.

If you are praying for the 'power' but you have no love in your heart, what is your agenda? Only the Holy Spirit can strengthen this love in us because it is the most important gift of all. It is the power of love that makes things happen. Everything you do must be based on love. These are the two New Testament commandments Jesus left with us:

"And Jesus replied to him, 'You shall love the Lord your God with all your heart, and with all your soul, and with all your mind.' This is the first and greatest commandment. The second is like it, 'You shall love your neighbour as yourself [that is, unselfishly seek the best or higher good for others].' The whole Law and the [writings of the] Prophets depend on these two commandments."

[Matthew 22:37-40 AMP]

For the Christian who is adamant that they have to live by the law and try to be perfect through their own efforts, try these two commandments and see how you get on. When God's love is perfect in you, you will know the truth, accept grace and no longer put yourself under the law. The Bible tells us many times that Jesus was so moved to compassion that He cried, and that, through that compassion, He did many miracles. The shortest scripture in the Bible encapsulates this love perfectly—John 11:35.

"Jesus wept."

Our God wept for us again and again. If you preach it and teach it, you must live it.

Strongholds

It would be very sad to think you are doing it God's way, that everything is right and you're on your way, only to find that somewhere along the way you make a wrong turn and never get back on track. Keep checking with the Lord that you are doing it right, that you are doing His will. He will correct you because He doesn't want you to fail. When your love for the Lord grows you will have a natural desire to do His will and find joy in it. When your love for the Lord starts growing cold, you will have a natural desire to follow your own will.

If you find yourself going back to the old you, struggling with the same things over and over again when you thought you had left them behind, these are known as strongholds. Those habits, feelings and behaviours can take a strong hold in you and, although you desire to live a righteous life, you may feel that you are failing because you can't quite shake them. The enemy will see this weakness and send his demonic forces to amplify it. He will try to make you feel like a failure or a hypocrite and try to convince you to give up. He will tell you 'this life is not really for you'. He is a liar. Don't listen to these thoughts—remember you are a new Christian learning the ways of the Lord, and this takes time.

Without becoming regimental and putting yourself under unnecessary stress and self-loathing, you should address the problem immediately. Start 'knocking on heaven's door'. In other words, start talking to the Lord about it. Enter into a season of fasting, prayer and reading the Bible. The Lord works with the desires of your heart and a desire that says, 'Lord, I need you; please help me, I can't do this by myself', is what the Lord wants to hear. He is your Father and He loves when you come to Him for help; never be afraid or ashamed. Tell the Lord that you are seeking His help and His strength for your problem and that you will be dedicating some time to come to him about the matter.

A prayer to help break strongholds:

My Father in heaven
Help me to get rid of the things that are not of you.
Help me to dig deep and bring to the surface what is lying beneath
Not to keep justifying my wrongdoings
And holding onto worldly pleasures in secret,
for nothing is secret to You.
Help me not to take advantage of your kindness with my
continuous sinning
And living a perpetual life of lies and deceit.
I cannot do this by myself, I cannot break this cycle.
Lord, You said Your strength is made perfect in my weakness.
The little things which were of no consequence are now stifling me
Unawares they took hold and are now taking over my will
Let my will be your will, Lord, I don't trust myself anymore.
Let Your will be done in my life.
I really need to change from this moment forward.
I am not prepared to live this way any more.
I cannot, I will not lose You.
I thank you wholeheartedly for all the things you have done for me
And for the things you continue to do for me
So please fill me with your strength.
I hand this situation over to You
In the name of Jesus
Amen.

Spiritual Gifts

Many spiritual gifts will be bestowed upon the Christian according to their purpose on Earth, but if they are not used for doing the will of God in the name of Jesus, these gifts will be for nothing. It doesn't matter how great you are on Earth, how many awards or Nobel Peace prizes you receive or how many special tributes are organised in your name—actually, that is the one of the problems right there, 'in your name'! Any praise or worship we receive as Christians must go to God. 'Why?,' you ask. Because without Him, we would be nothing and we would have no spiritual gifts. If He took the gifts away from us, we would have nothing. It is by God the Holy Spirit that Christians are able to heal the sick, raise the dead, prophesy, teach and do so much more.

Christians can and do go astray and start doing it 'their way'. Do not believe for a moment that everyone who is a Christian will enter into the kingdom of heaven. Nothing could be further from the truth. Remember, being a Christian in this life is the journey and not the destination. When you accept Jesus as your Lord and Saviour, you have not arrived, it's just the beginning.

"Not everyone who says to Me, 'Lord, Lord,' will enter the kingdom of heaven, but only he who does the will of My Father who is in heaven. Many will say to Me on that day [when I judge them], 'Lord, Lord, have we not prophesied in Your name, and driven out demons in Your name, and done many miracles in Your name?' And then I will declare to them publicly, 'I never knew you; depart from Me [you are banished from My presence], you who act wickedly [disregarding My commands].'"

[Matthew 7:21-23 AMP]

This scripture speaks solely about Christians who have been empowered by the Holy Spirit to do great things on the Earth, but who have used their gifts to seek earthly rewards and the praise of men. As they continue to work miracles on the Earth, their relationship with God breaks down and becomes non-existent. They revel in their works, their desires, their achievements, their self-righteousness and love for themselves and not in God. You may be asking why God did not take their gifts away from them, and this is a good question. Anything that God blesses you with, He will never take away from you. The gifts are irrevocable, amazing love!

"For the gifts and calling of God are without repentance." (KJV)

"For the gifts and the calling of God *are* irrevocable." (NKJV)

[Romans 11:29]

The King James Version of the Bible says these gifts are without repentance and the New King James Version tells us they are irrevocable, but their meanings are the same. When God blesses you, He really blesses you. If you do things that are wrong or walk away from the Lord, He does not take these gifts away from you. So, if you come back to Him and repent of your wrongdoings, you don't have to ask for your gifts to be re-instated, because you've always had them. Therefore, someone who is not living a good, righteous life can continue to prophesy, heal the sick, raise the dead, teach and preach, even though they no longer have a relationship with God. Clearly, we can see from the scriptures that this is not the place you want to find yourself.

The message here for the new Christian is not to be impressed with the things you see people doing. Be impressed by God and amazed by the wonders of Him and not 'man'. An indisputable rule of thumb is to stick close to the Holy Spirit. Check in regularly with Him if what you are doing is of Him. You cannot go wrong if you remain close to the Lord and nurture your relationship with Him.

This world is fickle and when you please 'man' they love you, but when you make a mistake they will seek to destroy you. God's love is consistent. It is tried and tested and we test it all the time. It has lasted from the beginning of time and it has not changed.

"For I am the LORD, I change not."

[Malachi 3:6 KJV]

If God took away His gifts from everyone who walked away from Him or misused them, there would be an argument on the day of judgement. When Jesus would say, 'What have you done with the gifts I bestowed on you?', they would say, 'Well, Lord, you took them away from me so I couldn't use them anymore.'

It is in our nature to shift the blame where possible and find excuses, so God is not going to help us to do that. If you think you are slipping a little too often or going back to the temptations you thought you had conquered, or are not sure if you are really doing the will of God, spend some time with Him.

It would be good for you to take a moment to read Matthew 7, the full chapter. It teaches us not to judge, that we must keep asking, seeking and knocking to get an answer from God. It identifies the two paths that Christians take—the narrow and wide paths—knowing who is for the Lord and who isn't and why some will not make it into heaven. The message here is to be wise and depend solely on Jesus, to leave the default position and to remain out of it.

The New Heaven

It is only right to give you a brief insight into the new heaven that many quibble over, whether they want to go there or not. When we step out of the default position and stay out of it, we cannot truly fathom the greatness of the gift of eternal life. The Lord promises that all things will be made new—the heaven and the Earth—at the end of this age. Everything as it is now will change. The book of Revelation (the last book in the Bible, written by the Apostle John) gives us an insight into the future.

"Then I saw a new heaven and a new earth; for the first heaven and the first earth had passed away [vanished], and there is no longer any sea. And I saw the holy city, new Jerusalem, coming down out of heaven from God, arrayed like a bride adorned for her husband; and then I heard a loud voice from the throne, saying, 'See! The tabernacle of God is among men, and He will live among them, and they will be His people, and God Himself will be with them [as their God] and He will wipe away every tear from their eyes; and there will no longer be death; there will no longer be sorrow and anguish, or crying, or pain; for the former order of things has passed away.'"

[Revelation 21:1-4 AMP]

This sad, broken world will exist no more. No depression or despair, no more suffering or death. God will live with His people once more, the ones who accepted Jesus as their Lord and Saviour. "I saw no temple in it, for the Lord God Almighty [the Omnipotent, the Ruler of all] and the Lamb are its temple. And the city has no need of the sun nor of the moon to give light to it, for the glory [splendour, radiance] of God has illumined it, and the Lamb is its lamp and light. The nations [the redeemed people from the earth] will walk by its light, and the kings of the earth will bring into it their glory. By day (for there will be no night there) its gates will never be closed [in fear of evil]; and they will bring the glory [splendour, majesty] and the honour of the nations into it.

[Revelation 21:22-26 AMP]

That is truly a world worth fighting for!

Recommended Reading

Matthew Chapter 7   Jesus Teaches Us How to Live

ACTIVITY 14

Why did Lot's wife turn into a pillar of salt? ....

....

....

....

The Lord works with the outward appearance. True or False?..........

....

Where will the new heaven be located?...

....

What is a stronghold?...

....

....

....

Can you identify any strongholds in your life?...................................

....

....

Notes: ....

This World of Confusion

This world is a melting pot of confusion
One minute it's this, the next it's that
Now in great health, then you're not
That saying we hear, but take little notice of
'In the midst of life, we are in death'
Is really so true…
But to dwell on it would make you blue.

Wars, rumours of wars and threats
Leave little room for sober thoughts
Joy comes hand-in-hand with sadness
And no one can escape their wilderness.
Then loneliness and pain take over
Wondering if it will ever end
Daring to hope as you continue to fend

For yourself against the relentless attacks
Of the enemy using those both near and far
Enemies and loved ones he attracts
Enticing with lies and seduction
Leaving in his wake a trail of destruction
When? When will this madness end?
Not yet! We must endure
For a little more

And wait, wait and watch so as not to be late
Being careful not to be left at the gate
Looking to the wedding supper
When we'll be called home
No more pain, hurt or confusion
Replaced by a glorious infusion
Of peace, love and happiness
To bow before His Royal Highness!

CHAPTER 15
DON'T WALK AWAY

"Do not be overcome and conquered by evil, but overcome evil with good."

Romans 12:21 AMP

Evil must never win in the life of a Christian. We must respond to all evils by doing good and we must never let evil win in our lives. To fight evil with evil is to become the very thing we are fighting against. Christians who walk away from the Lord for whatever reason, who stay away from Him and die without Him, have allowed themselves to be overcome by evil. This is one of the two worst things that could ever happen to a Christian. The other will be mentioned later.

To walk away from a holy life and go back to living an unholy one is to 'backslide'. This term is used primarily in the book of Jeremiah [2:19, 31:22, 49:4 KJV and NKJV] and refers to the lapse of the nation of Israel into paganism and idolatry. It is to lapse and slip back into an immoral lifestyle, to completely walk away from your faith, to revert back to the 'old you' and the old ways, allowing yourself to be corrupted by sin once again. If this happens you have 'backslidden'. No one needs to confirm this for you; you will know if you are no longer living a holy life.

The Lord is deeply saddened by this, but He is still there for you if you have a desire to return and re-dedicate your life to Him; He will open His arms to you in a heartbeat. The world does not understand God's unconditional love, so it struggles to accept that it is that simple to come to the Lord or to come back to Him. Remember, He has forgiven past, present and future sins, but you have to access that forgiveness and activate it in your life by asking for it. Consequences of backsliding and dying in that state are mentioned in the following scripture:

"For if after they have escaped the pollutions of the world through the knowledge of the Lord and Saviour Jesus Christ, they are again entangled therein, and overcome, the latter end is worse with them than the beginning. For it had been better for them not to have known the way of righteousness, than, after they have known it, to turn from the holy commandment delivered unto them."

[2 Peter 2:20-21 NKJV]

For anyone who knows the Lord, has received of His love and forgiveness, was cleaned up by the Holy Spirit and yet chooses to go back to the world and rejects the Lord once again, then on the day of judgement the punishment will be more severe than for someone who had never known Him at all. The Lord does not walk away from us, it is we who walk away from Him.

For some reason, many people don't seem to understand the seriousness of the situation, so let's take a moment to reflect on the message we are sending to the Lord.

REFLECTION

If someone loved you with all their heart, to the point of dying for you, and you promised to love them for life, but left them after a short time to be with another (one who could not possibly love you to any degree but who seeks always to destroy you and yours), would you expect to be rewarded for this or would you expect consequences?

Would you expect to receive the same reward as the faithful ones who worked at their relationship with God and endured to the end? There are consequences for every action throughout our lives, even if we don't know it at the time. You cannot go through life without being responsible for your actions. Some consequences can be dealt with and you can survive them, but others you can't.

When we make a vow to follow the Lord, He takes it very seriously and so should we. When we turn away from that vow, He takes it equally as seriously, but His mercy allows us to come back to Him at any time and He will not hold our error against us. The simple steps back would be to acknowledge your wrongdoings, repent of your actions, ask the Lord to forgive you and follow Him with all your heart. A simple prayer could be:

Father, I know I have sinned and walked away from you. Please forgive me. I wholeheartedly re-dedicate my life to you. I ask for your strength to help me not to fail You again.
I thank You for Your grace and mercy.
I ask this in the name of my Lord and Saviour Jesus Christ.
Amen.

But life is never that simple and the way back is far from easy. No matter how many times you return to the Lord throughout your journey, He will forgive you and take you back. Walking away from Him puts you back in that default position, regardless of whether you convince yourself that you are a good person or not.

Many Christians who walk away from the Lord try to justify their position by saying 'I still love the Lord in my heart' or 'I don't have to go to church to prove that I'm a Christian'. If you reject Christ, you have accepted the devil, even if you did not make a conscious decision to do so—it really is that simple. It is the rejection of Christ that will result in an eternity without Him—an eternity you do not want to be a part of. An eternity of remembering everything but never being able to do anything about it, living with regret and knowing you had the joy of eternal peace and you let it go.

It is a really, really sad situation and the only person to blame would be yourself and not God. It's not the parents who abused you, nor the Christian who victimised you, nor the terrorists who persecuted you—just you! As harshly as this reads, it is the truth. God will heal you from everything if you let Him, but many prefer to hold onto their anger and hatred. This may be justifiable to man but not to God. We have a choice and free will to make that choice. If anyone has defects from birth or anything that may prevent them from understanding the gospel enough to make a choice to follow Christ, then we have to trust that the Lord has a plan in place for this and not spend a lifetime wondering about something we have no control over. Remember, your faith is a complete trust in God!

This subject is expansive and very deep, but if you take nothing else away from this chapter, please take the fact that you will be judged more harshly than someone who had never known Christ at all. This is because you experienced His love and all He had to offer and rejected Him anyway.

As Christians we refer to this as 'putting Christ back on the cross', because He died for us, and we said thank you, accepted Him, then walked away, so what was the point of Him dying for us?

Your personal journey will be difficult, make no mistake about it. There will be many pressures and injuries along the way. There will be many variables all coming into play: the pressures of life, spiritual challenges and attacks from family, friends and strangers alike, but God will give you the strength to go through any struggles if you let Him.

"No temptation [regardless of its source] has overtaken or enticed you that is not common to human experience [nor is any temptation unusual or beyond human resistance]; but God is faithful [to His word—He is compassionate and trustworthy], and He will not let you be tempted beyond your ability [to resist], but along with the temptation He [has in the past and is now and] will [always] provide the way out as well, so that you will be able to endure it [without yielding, and will overcome temptation with joy]."

[1 Corinthians 10:13 AMP]

Know that God has already made a way for you to escape from your struggles as long as you don't give up. A word of caution though, the escape route you may have planned for yourself won't be the same one that God has planned for you. Your timescales will not be God's timescales, because He transcends our time. God does not do things the way we do and we cannot do things the way He does, so we must just trust Him to bring us through.

Sometimes you may find yourself in the default position again without realising it. Other times you may make a conscious decision to put yourself back in it and try to ignore the consequences. Some remain very aware of the consequences every single day without ever really doing anything to change the situation. This is no life at all, living 'in limbo', not fully committing to either life and living neither of them very well. Yearning for one but living the other. You have only two options: remain in the life you have chosen or find your way back.

Limbo

I myself lived in limbo for some twenty-five years, having walked away from the Lord, and I can tell you the way back was not easy. My Christian journey started some thirty-three years ago in Jamaica in 1983, at the age of nineteen, but my life with the Lord started a long time before then. Ever since I can remember, I have always had a deep unwavering belief in God. I had a challenging childhood and a very strict upbringing with its ups, downs and extremes. When it was good it was very good (though this was rare) and when it was bad it was very bad, but I endured.

My parents brought me up to believe in God and, although they weren't regular churchgoers themselves, they encouraged us (me and my siblings) to go to church, which we did without them. We had many family devotions at home, especially at Christmas and Easter, and Jesus was actively discussed in our household. These solid beginnings never left me and later shaped my life.

I prayed a lot, learning the Lord's Prayer and Psalm 23 from a very early age along with the books and many stories of the Bible. I can't remember how or when I learnt these things, but it was definitely before the age of eight as that was my age when I moved to England and I knew them before I arrived. Born in Jamaica to Jamaican parents, I lived there until my parents brought me and my other siblings to live with them in England.

I read the Bible throughout my young life and spoke to God all the time, asking Him questions like "How were you born, God?", "Where are you from?", "Who created you?", "How can we live for ever and ever?", "What do You look like?", until I'd exhausted and scared myself. When I was sad, I would tell God about it, often in tears, and when I was happy I would share my joy with Him. When I was challenged by life and uncertain about making decisions, I would look up into the sky, often at night, and talk to Him about it in my heart. Sometimes I would speak out loud if I was alone.

I grew up believing that everyone spoke to God that way, so imagine the shock and the rude awakening I had at the age of thirteen when I found out that, in fact, everyone does not speak to God and some don't even believe that He exists. My religious education teacher decided to tell the class one day after we'd pushed her too far (by refusing to stop talking) that she didn't believe in God. It was just a job to her and, if we didn't want to learn, that was up to us.

Well, she got my attention then. To say I was shocked is an understatement. I was horrified and spent the rest of the lesson in silent thought and disbelief. I had many discussions with my parents, who clearly were not surprised by the declaration, and I tried to comprehend what she'd really meant by it, beginning to understand the real world that I lived in.

So, having talked to God as far back as I can remember, it was a natural progression to become a Christian. I really hadn't set out to do it; it happened through a sequence of unplanned events.

When my parents decided to return to Jamaica, in the family there was much excitement. We emigrated in March 1983, three months before my nineteenth birthday. As a family we had grown apart: two siblings had left home, our parents were not happy together and those of us who remained at home looked forward to leaving and going out into the big wide world.

After arriving in Jamaica, I too decided that the pressures of home life with extremely strict parents were too much to bear and decided to leave four months later. On the night I left I had nowhere to go but to a friend of the family who had a small room at the end of their garden, where I stayed for the night. The next morning, one of my cousins picked me up and took me to the home where he lived with his adopted mother and her family. Wouldn't you know it, she was a Christian.

She took me in and treated me as part of the family; going to church with them was calming to my restless spirit. Church was a small 'tent', not yet a building, but it served its purpose. It consisted of a cement floor and outer posts with canvas around the sides and top, giving the appearance of a tent. It had a pulpit for preaching and seating for the musicians and the choir. There was a separate building in the grounds for the offices and church administration. Services were absolutely wonderful and I felt a real freedom and joy in my spirit when worshipping. Needless to say, no one had to prompt or encourage me to give my life to the Lord.

After I'd been going for a few months, my hand shot straight up when the Pastor asked if anyone wanted to accept the Lord Jesus as their Saviour, and I was baptised at the next scheduled baptism. It was the best time of my young life. I would walk to and from church any hour of the day or night without a thought or concern about my safety and the usual things we worry ourselves with in life. I had no traumatic experiences and it never occurred to me that I could.

I think it is worth noting here that sometimes as Christians we try to do too much and try to do the work of the Holy Spirit for Him by pressuring people to become Christians. Once you witness to someone, share Jesus with them, show them love and kindness and they worship with you, they have to make the decision to follow the Lord for themselves. Constant pressure and probing questions, making someone feel uncomfortable and forced into it, will not enable their faith to stand the test of time. If they do it for the wrong reasons, if the new convert's faith is not truly in Jesus Christ, they have not been saved and you have done them a disservice.

The Holy Spirit is perfectly capable of working with their hearts and drawing them, and they will commit when they are ready…or not.

My newly adopted family took me to church, witnessed to me, answered all my questions and showed me love. I was never asked, 'What are you waiting for?', 'When are you going to be baptised?' or 'Why didn't you go church today?' There was no pressure at all and, on hearing the Word preached, reading my Bible, asking questions and opening my heart to the Lord I made the decision to be baptised.

It was a joyous occasion. As I had left home, none of my family members were there to share it with me, but the church was full and my new family was there—it was great! Two to three months later

I went to a church convention in Kingston, and when the altar call was made for anyone wanting to receive the Baptism of the Holy Spirit they didn't have to ask me twice.

A little uncertain of what to expect, I made my way to the altar, knelt and prayed, asking the Lord to 'fill me', and He did. As I knelt there, I had a vision of the woman with the issue of blood pressing through the crowd to get to Jesus. I saw the back of Jesus as He walked and I was then in the crowd behind Him. As I reached my hand up (I actually did this as I knelt on the floor) to touch the hem of His garment, I was filled with the Baptism of the Holy Spirit and the tongues flowed to the point where I could not stop myself.

The experience was amazing and I felt elated. I can tell you that it was not by my effort but by God's grace and the promise He made to us that He would send the Comforter. I didn't do anything special. I didn't spend weeks in fasting and prayer (not that there is anything wrong with that), I wasn't any more or less worthy than anyone else. I asked for it from the bottom of my heart because I believed that God would do what He said He would, and at no point did I doubt Him.

Worship services were awesome and I especially looked forward to the moving of the Holy Spirit when we would speak in tongues and some would interpret and our spirits were totally refreshed and empowered.

But life continued and personal circumstances dictated my return to England. I was immediately concerned because, although I had every intention of continuing as a Christian, I knew no other Christians in England. I knew no churches because I grew up in Derby but was returning to Nottingham. Also, having experienced the Holy Spirit, I wanted to find a church where Christians believed in the Holy Spirit, and this wasn't the case with the small local churches we had attended as children. The churches I had visited as a child were very quiet, orthodox churches, quite different from the joyous nature of the Pentecostal churches.

The only person I knew in Nottingham was my older sister, who was instrumental in my return. Before I'd left Jamaica, I had been given the name and address of the nearest church in our network of churches.

I was twenty, back in England and living with my older sister in a lovely two-bedroom flat in the centre of Nottingham City, and was, for the first time in my life, away from any parental or authoritative control. I could do whatever I wanted and dress however I pleased, which to be fair really wasn't anything outrageous or out of the ordinary. I didn't know where to find the church that had been recommended to me or which bus to take and I certainly didn't want to go on my own, having been a painful introvert from birth.

I had always found it easier to talk to God than to people. So the first Sunday morning I was due to venture out into a new city to find the church came and went. It was a very cold September morning and I decided to stay in bed and go the following week. The following weeks came and went until I stopped trying. Then the guilt set in and this continued for a while until I realised that I really didn't want to do this on my own. I missed my very happy life in Jamaica, I missed going to church with my adopted family and I missed the warmth of the weather and the people.

I was cold all the time and I wasn't enjoying life. There was no one to share this with who would understand, so I kept it to myself. Eventually I made friends who were not Christians and they started inviting me out to clubs and parties. I started meeting new people and dating and getting on with life back in the default position, but always aware of the choices I was making.

It was a very confusing time for me. Sometimes I would wear something to a party, trying very hard to fit in, and would receive funny stares and the odd snigger because I looked more like I was going to church than to an all-night party.

You don't realise that, when you are a Christian, you are perceived by others as being different. You even act differently, often without realising it. When you go back into the world, it takes some worldly training to fit in again and the enemy will surround you with the people to do it. My re-training, or training to be more accurate, began. Having been brought up by strict parents meant that my siblings and I did not 'do' parties and clubs. We hardly drank, never smoked and rarely socialised as most teenagers did. So my social life started at the age of twenty with an awkwardness that came from not knowing the ways of the world.

Throughout this time, I continued to speak to the Lord, because I was fully aware of the path I was taking. I told Him that I was sorry I didn't have the strength to keep going in the faith, and I asked Him never to leave me because one day I would be back. I asked Him not to let me die before I was able to get back to Him and truly believed that I would one day return to His grace. It was a stressful life in limbo. I said this prayer and variations of it for the duration of the twenty-five years or so that I remained in the default position.

I continued to pray, read my Bible (occasionally), started going to churches on an ad hoc basis, often made New Year's resolutions to get back into the faith, but never followed through. I continued living according to my will and my efforts, knowing that if I left the world at any point during that time, I would not be going to heaven.

We are a stubborn people, so for anyone working with people still 'in the world' or 'backsliders', the sledgehammer approach really doesn't work. It is the desire of the person and the working of the Holy Spirit that will win out. Others can be an example, guide, encourage and be there for someone, but they can't force them or get angry with them; it doesn't work. They may already be feeling guilty and torn, so they will reject the forcefulness of others.

Knowing the Lord, walking away from Him and trying to live without Him is not easy and I often thought of myself as living in 'limbo'. The backslider (and I really disliked being called a backslider, but it is what it is) is no longer covered under the blood of Jesus. It doesn't matter how good a life you think you are living, or how much you claim to still love Him in your heart—if you are not committed to Him and living according to the Word of God, everything you do is futile.

It is not an easy road finding your way back because your own efforts and strength are not enough. There is a real spiritual battle going on in and around you and only the power of the Holy Spirit can break through. You must seek to get back into a relationship with Jesus and He will work with the desires of your heart. As long as you continue to live in the world without Him, there will be a void that cannot be filled by anything in that life. Where the Holy Spirit once dwelt, nothing and no one can take His place; it is empty and you have a void. You are painfully aware that something is missing in your life because there is no other love like it.

Some people who return to the world try very hard to fill that void, to stop feeling the conviction of the Holy Spirit when He reminds them of their faith and who they are, so they resort to a life that is so far removed from the Christian life that a journey back is extremely difficult, though not impossible. This is not because the Lord won't take them back, it is because they refuse to ask Him. In doing so they repress the memories of that good life, get angry when Christians try to support them and refuse to visit churches, even for weddings and christenings. They don't want to deal with anything or anyone that reminds them of their faith. And, of course, you know the devil is in the detail, because he sends his most skilled demonic spirits to surround them and work on them to keep them in that default position: sin.

The following scripture explains what happens in the spiritual realm when someone is cleaned up from the world and then goes back into it:

"When the unclean spirit comes out of a person, it roams through waterless places in search [of a place] of rest; and not finding any, it says, 'I will go back to my house [person] from which I came.' And when it comes, it finds the place swept and put in order. Then it goes and brings seven other spirits more evil than itself, and they go in [the person] and live there; and the last state of that person becomes worse than the first."

[Luke 11:24-26 AMP]

The devil is not the creator. He cannot create anything, he can only use what is already available to him. These are the same old tricks he uses to manipulate and break someone and, unfortunately, we allow him to do so. He sends spirits to possess and oppress us, and only when we accept the Lord and those spirits leave us are we cleansed and able to live righteous lives.

However, those spirits that have left us are not at rest. They didn't want to leave us, but when the Holy Spirit stepped in they had no choice. They will keep trying to come back into our life, or 'our house' as the scripture refers to us, though if we are still clean and living righteous lives there is nothing they can do but go away again. The problem is when these spirits come to check out how we are doing and find that we have gone back out into the world and 'the house' is empty and prepared for a different occupant—that we are no longer living for the Lord. Then the spirits go and fetch reinforcements, who are stronger than they are, to dwell in and around us, to possess and oppress us; and this time, their hold on us is even stronger than before.

When this happens, a strategic plan is being executed by a team of demonic spirits working to keep you in the world. When you try to come back to the Lord from here, you will find yourself dealing with all kinds of worldly temptations and challenges; even things that may not have been much of a challenge for you previously suddenly become stumbling blocks. Telling yourself that you don't need to get back to the Lord, that you are doing alright by yourself and you will worship in your heart, are lies from the enemy. Ask the Lord to help you to find your way back. Only when you know the game can you change it. Ask the Lord to remove all these spirits that are around you, controlling your will, and identify the things of the world that are keeping you tied to it and call them out in your prayers. Ask the Lord to loosen the spirits' grip on you, and He will step into your situation to guide you and bring you out. There will be a battle, that's a given. It will be relentless—but, if you hold fast to the knowledge that God will bring you through, then you will win.

Anyone living this life in limbo and thinking they are alright because they still love God in their heart, and claiming to know what they are doing, is actually bound up by the enemy more than they realise. God has not made an arrangement with Satan that His (God's) people can love Him in their hearts but that Satan can control their lives and they can live as they please in the world. The following scripture tells us clearly that we cannot serve two masters:

"No servant can serve two masters: for either he will hate the one, and love the other; or else he will hold to the one, and despise the other. You cannot serve God and mammon [money, greed, ambition]."

[Luke 16:13 KJV]

Good and evil are worlds apart, and if you try to live in both worlds, you will end up treating one master worse than the other according to your personal desires.

If I had died during my twenty-five years away from the Lord, I would definitely have gone straight to Hades (a hell in the underworld, somewhere hot and miserable to await the final judgement)—I knew it and feared it. I would not have had an argument on judgement day and neither will you if you turn your back on the Lord. My judgement would also have been harsher than a sinner who had never known God, and so will yours if you turn your back on the Lord. Again, this is not to scare you, just to present facts supported by scripture and to pray that these words will emphasise the urgency with which you need to find your way back to the Lord.

I had a real yearning and a longing to be back with the Lord, but somehow wasn't able to take that step on my own. I was never sure why, because there was nothing great in the world that I was holding onto. I kept telling the Lord, 'I will be back one day, I just don't know when', and I told Him that, although I didn't know when, I knew He did because He could see into my heart and into the future.

The bottom started falling out of my world and everything that could go wrong started going wrong. When the enemy has lulled you into a false sense of security and made you think that you are all 'sorted', that you're having a great life and that you've got there all by yourself, it is then that he pulls the rug out from under you and tears apart everything in your life.

Often when a bad thing happens in people's lives they say it comes in threes and they expect other things to start going wrong. This is the enemy's plan of attack, to snatch away all you hold dear; and it's not in threes, it is a calculated, strategic and sustained plan of attack to completely break you. The one-off mishap here and there won't do it and the enemy knows this; he will throw everything at you all at once.

It is at this point that people start losing hope. Their job is gone, their house is gone, their marriage is broken, their friends are gone, there have been sickness and accidents.

At this point, you will be wondering what is going on. Although you will be hurt, confused, angry and broken, you can turn the situation around and cry out to God. Remember, He is omnipresent (in all places at the same time) and omnipotent (an awesome power that we cannot comprehend). No one can overpower Him. Some people feel guilty and decide that, because they are only turning to God when something has gone wrong, they can't turn to Him. Wrong! You can turn to God at any time. The idea that we can't is our way of thinking, not God's way of thinking.

When the bottom started falling out of my world, I recognised the game of the enemy; it was unnatural. At work, my contracts were being cancelled for silly reasons, interviews were not productive, there were plots in the workplace to attack my work and much scheming in the background to discredit me. Anyone who attempted to defend me had their contract cancelled as well. It was a very surreal feeling. I refused to go to anyone for help because I knew they couldn't help me, so I went to the one person who could, my Father in heaven, and started talking to Him more than ever.

I became very determined to find my way back. I sat on my sofa one day and asked the Lord some serious questions in my spirit (I didn't vocalise them). I asked Him about my life and how different it would have been if I had stayed with Him. Three days later my sister Marie (also a Christian), who lived several miles away and had absolutely no idea about this, rang me out of the blue and said she had a message for me from the Lord. This is how great God is: she called me with the answer from the Lord. Awesome!

The message from the Lord was, "Seek first the kingdom of God and His righteousness and all these things shall be added unto you" [Matthew 6:33]. That was the answer to my questions and I knew it the moment I heard it, so I shared this with my sister, telling her that I had asked God some questions and this was the answer.

I had already made up my mind to get back to the Lord and had truly done it in my heart for a while but had not openly re-dedicated my life to Him. After some discussion, Marie encouraged me to get back under the covering of the blood of Jesus. I had been talking to the Lord about it a lot and had decided to visit her church and a couple of others to find one where I would like to worship.

God's forgiveness is readily available to those who ask for it and, true to His Word, He forgave me and has never reminded me of it again, though I do sometimes reflect on the dangerous situation I was in where I could have lost my soul for all eternity. I don't dwell on it, but my reflections are a sharp reminder never to allow myself to get back into that situation. The following scripture reassures me of His promise to forgive me:

"If we confess our sins, he is faithful and just to forgive us our sins, and to cleanse us from all unrighteousness."

[1 John 1:9 NKJV]

The enemy will bring it back to you and try to make you feel guilty about it, but the Bible tells us there is no guilt or condemnation in Christ Jesus, so we should take comfort in this and dismiss it from our thoughts.

People walk away from the Lord for so many reasons that it is impossible to list them all. Some are bruised by religious practices, others have been treated unfairly by a member or members of the church, some are tempted back into the world by the things they miss, whilst others weaken in their faith and fall away. Whatever the reason, we are all still responsible for our walk with the Lord and ultimately our salvation. Blaming someone else will not be an excuse on the day of judgement. We must forgive or we will not be forgiven. Forgiveness releases us from the situation as much as the person we are forgiving. If we do not forgive and let it go, we bind ourselves into that situation and cannot move on.

FACT

If you have been hurt by someone, Christian or not, and walk away from the Lord as a result of it, dying without ever coming back to Him, you will end up in an eternity without Him. If, however, the person who offended you and inflicted this pain later repents, asks for forgiveness and follows the Lord until death, they will go to heaven, whilst you will not. My point here is, wouldn't it be very sad that you allowed someone to cause you to lose your salvation whilst they kept theirs?

God is no respecter of persons and anyone who asks for forgiveness will receive it. Also, if the other person does not repent and you both end up in a miserable eternity, wouldn't it be horrible to be in the same place as the person who caused you pain, whom you labelled as being evil or cruel, only to realise you were no better than them? Would you really want to spend an eternity dealing with that? Probably wondering why, if you were a good person who harmed no one, how did you end up in that place with the wicked?

Parable of the Father

Jesus used little stories known as parables to get a point across, so following His example, I will use a little story to explain how pointless it is to let someone else cause you to lose your salvation and how unnatural it is to blame God.

There was a father who was very wealthy and had eight children whom he brought up by himself after the death of his wife. He loved them, nurtured and cherished them, giving them everything to ensure they had a good life. When they were old enough, they left home to have families of their own and he became a grandfather and great-grandfather. They would all visit him regularly for family gatherings as well as weddings, birthdays, Christmases and Easter celebrations. They all had a great relationship with each other. He was always there for his family, helping and supporting them to deal with the good and the bad.

One day, two of his daughters had a disagreement and, through a series of events, one ended up losing her job, which put stress on her marriage, whilst the other continued to thrive in her endeavours. The situation remained unresolved and neither would speak to the other. The father gave the best advice he could to both daughters and supported them where he could; however, as they were grown now with children of their own, he also had to let them make their own decisions. The daughter who was the instigator and had caused the rift made efforts to reconcile with her sister and continued to have a close relationship with her father and the other members of the family. The sister who had been wounded by the experience remained angry, rejected her father and family, broke contact and moved away. She refused to accept any invitations from her father, would not speak to him, refused to allow her children to visit him and never rebuilt her relationship with him or any other member of her family.

Many years later when her father died, she turned up for his funeral. She was a stranger to everyone, had nothing in common with them, her children didn't know their family and the situation was awkward at best. There was no special place for her at the table and she received no inheritance. She was alone and hurt but there was nothing she could do about it; it was too late. He was gone and she could not reclaim those years but lived on with the memories and the hurt while everyone else had moved on. She lost out on not just her inheritance, but an amazing life with her father and her family and all the rewards inherent in that life.

One daughter lost all her inheritance because she couldn't forgive and move past the hurt. If you have been hurt by a member of your church or another Christian, whether they seek to resolve the issue or not, please don't lose your inheritance from God because of them. It doesn't make sense to have a bad experience with someone, blame God and then sever your relationship with Him and the other members of your church or other Christians from other churches who have done you no harm. It is flawed reasoning.

In your spiritual walk, you will need to reflect on your reasons and whether you have been looking for a way out in your heart and are using the situation as an excuse to walk away from your faith. God will know this, because we can fool others but we cannot fool Him, and we are not really fooling ourselves. You should never walk away from the Lord and refuse to speak to Him or to assemble with your fellow Christians in the house of God because of an injustice against you. Remember, God will use the situation to train and strengthen you—if you let Him.

Everyone struggles with injustice, but no one can claim a greater injustice against them than Jesus Christ, and He said on the cross before He died at the hands of His own, "Father, forgive them for they know not what they do" [Luke 23:34 KJV]. Whatever the injustice, go to the Lord with it—all of it. Offload on Him and let Him help you and build you back up so you can be prepared for the next one, for the Christian will experience many injustices on their journey.

This journey is about winning the battles and not the war. The war is for God and He has already won it. We just need to survive.

The Unforgiveable Sin

So, the first worst thing to happen to a Christian, as we have just discussed, is to walk away from God. The second worst thing is to commit the only sin that God will not forgive, to blaspheme the Holy Spirit. A lot of new Christians are nervous when they hear of it, thinking they have committed the unforgiveable sin. I have stated many times that God forgives every sin, so it's time to explain what this really means.

I have chosen not to mention this one before now so as not to cause confusion, because this sin can only be committed by someone who knows exactly what they are doing and why they are doing it. It can only be committed by someone who knows the workings of God the Holy Spirit and still chooses to deny Him or claim that His work is the working of the devil, as the scribes and the Pharisees did. This is a person whose heart has become so dark, who wrestles against the works of God so continuously, that the Lord can't do anything with them and, quite frankly, who doesn't want the Lord to do anything with them.

As the world does not know the Holy Spirit, when they sin it is usually against God and Jesus. They always deny the Holy Spirit because they refuse to believe that He exists, and this is not the unforgiveable sin. Jesus tells us about the unforgiveable sin:

"'I assure you and most solemnly say to you, all sins will be forgiven the sons of men, and all the abusive and blasphemous things they say; but whoever blasphemes against the Holy Spirit and His power [by attributing the miracles done by Me to Satan] never has forgiveness, but is guilty of an everlasting sin [a sin which is unforgivable in this present age as well as in the age to come].' Because the scribes and Pharisees were [attributing His miracles to Satan by] saying, 'He has an unclean spirit.'"

[Mark 3:28-30 AMP]

There is such a sin, and that is to accuse the Holy Spirit of being an unclean spirit. It is to attribute the works of the Holy Spirit to the devil. To fully understand how and why this might happen is to take a step back into the Old Testament and follow the journey of Christ.

Throughout the Old Testament, from the book of Genesis when mankind fell, God tells us that Jesus will come. The coming of the Messiah, the Son of God, was prophesied again and again. It was taught to the Jewish nation through Judaism (their faith), as Christianity did not exist at this time. The Jewish leaders studied, taught and lived by the scriptures.

When Jesus was born, His greatest challenge came from the very people who had studied and taught their communities about Him for centuries, passing them down from generation to generation. The scribes, Pharisees and Sadducees were the Jewish religious leaders who refused to accept Jesus because He was not born in a palace like the earthly kings and He did not come to do their will, which was to challenge the rule of the Romans.

They had their own idea of how the Messiah should come and what He should do to save them and they refused to accept God's will. Their hearts were so dark and hardened against God's plan that they challenged everything that was done through the Holy Spirit, ultimately declaring that they were the workings of the devil. They plotted, planned, lied, bribed, and when that didn't work, they made up their own stories. No amount of preaching, teaching or miracles could convince them. Not even the raising of the dead, which they witnessed! There was nothing God could do with them.

"Then a demon-possessed man who was blind and mute was brought to Jesus, and He healed him, so that the mute man both spoke and saw. All the people wondered in amazement, and said, 'Could this be the Son of David [the Messiah]?' But the Pharisees heard it and said, 'This man casts out demons only by [the help of] Beelzebub [Satan] the prince of the demons.'

[Matthew 12:22-24 AMP]

The Pharisees were fearful because the people were beginning to believe in Jesus, so they increased their efforts to reject Him by claiming that He was casting out demons by the power of a demonic spirit. And not just any demon but the ruler of the demons, because the miracles were so powerful.

We all know by now that the ruler of the demons is Satan, who is the devil, the evilest spirit ever to exist. The Pharisees attributed the power, goodness and grace of God and His healing power to a demonic spirit when they knew the truth. The fact that they knew the truth is what sets this sin apart from every other sin of the world.

The moment they did this they committed the sin from which there is no return and no forgiveness. To be sure, they did not even bother to ask for forgiveness. They were so arrogant and prideful that they completely disregarded the power of God and refused to acknowledge that there would be consequences for their actions. They absolutely refused to be corrected, even after they killed our Lord. They showed no remorse and continued to concoct stories about how His body was stolen from the tomb, denying that He had risen. So, again, you can see here that, when someone blasphemes the Holy Spirit, their heart is so evil, dark and unrepentant that God cannot get through to them and He will not force them to change.

When someone sees the Spirit of God working, whether through a specific person or otherwise, and attributes this to the devil, it is that sin that God will not forgive. The simple lesson to learn here is never to attribute anything of God to the devil. Recognise the things of God!

What If…?
Many are adamant that there is no greater power than us, no creator of the universe, no God, nothing after death; we just die and then there is no more consciousness, nothing. It is as if we never existed. If you truly believe this, I have a question for you. What if you are wrong? What if there really is a God and everything He has taught us is true and there really is a heaven and a hell and an eternal life after the physical death?

You may be asking at the same time, what if I am wrong? What if the Bible is wrong? Well, if I am wrong then we live, we die and we all rest in peace with no more consciousness, no heaven, no hell and all is well. If I am wrong, I lose nothing, but if you are wrong, you lose everything. There will be no rest in peace but a life of eternal unrest. It is in everyone's best interest not to accept only what the natural eye sees but to seek the truth for themselves. Be curious, question everything!

The world invests a lot of time in trying to prove that God does not exist—a God it does not believe existed in the first place—so why put so much effort into it? Surely if someone believes that there is no God that should be sufficient for them, but this is clearly not the case. How many expensive and time-consuming experiments have been attempted, by very intelligent and learned experts, to work out how Jesus performed miracles they don't believe ever happened, or whether or not Noah's Ark ever existed, or whether Pharaoh and his army actually drowned in the Red Sea?

Why spend their lives trying to prove something they don't believe ever existed in the first place? It doesn't make sense to me, unless there is an element in there somewhere that is not sitting right with them, something that keeps tugging at their spirit or challenging their disbelief. It is my belief that many people who say they do not believe there is a God actually do believe to some extent, but choose to reject the truth because it is not what they want in their lives or it doesn't sit well with their logic.

To believe in God, let Him guide us and give Him control in our lives is just too much for many people to accept. People like control and power. They enjoy boasting of their personal achievements and the self-gratifying feeling that they did it all by themselves. They walked on the moon, conquered a race, discovered a planet—they are the greatest that ever lived. And the thought of saying, 'I was able to do this through the strength and empowerment of Jesus Christ' is too much to accept.

I cannot imagine a more wasted existence than to believe that someone or something doesn't exist, but to then spend my entire life trying to *prove* that it really doesn't exist.

Jesus is definitely returning to us very soon, but many people either don't believe it or think it is still a long way away. Remember, Christ left us just over two days ago by God's time, so will it be another half day, a few more hours, a week? We don't know. We need to be alert and not ignore the signs of the times.

Deal-breaker

Many Christians fall away from the faith and many people refuse to come to it because of a fundamental lack of understanding. For the Christian, injustice is often a deal-breaker due to this lack of understanding. The Christian journey sets you apart from the world, and anyone set apart from the world lives in it but is no longer a part of it. Therefore, if you no longer take part in worldly practices, don't expect to be accepted by the players in that game.

Not only may they not want you to eat at the same table as them, but they could also victimise you, sometimes openly but more often subtly. The workplace is a fertile ground for this. Your strategy is to expect it, armour up with the right spiritual tools, talk to the Lord about it (a lot), and let Him deal with it for you.

This does not mean you will not have to go through the struggles inherent in these situations, because you must. When a baby is learning to walk they fall over many times. A parent will try to catch them when it first starts happening, but they cannot prevent it; otherwise the baby will never learn to walk.

Many of us come to the Lord believing that everyone who is called has love in their hearts for God and for each other and that now they are in church all will be well and everyone will welcome them with open arms. Unfortunately, this is not always the case. The first few years in the life of a Christian are hugely important in much the same way as the first few years in the life of a baby. A good start in a new life lays solid foundations, and a bad start will hinder progress and cause unnecessary pain because the foundations are not solid.

Love

Becoming a Christian is the first step on the journey, not the destination. Love started us on this journey and love will bring us through. Often when relationships fail in life, you will hear people say, 'Love was not enough'. This belief is expressed in films and books again and again.

While this statement is true to some extent, it is not the whole story. The truth is, our love is not enough but God's love is more than enough and perfectly able to cope with anything we experience in life. We need to practise God's unfailing, unconditional, unfathomable, transcendent love. Through it, all things can be accomplished.

It may seem a little strange when I say to practise loving people, especially when they do evil things to you, but that is the single most important factor that will keep you flowing in your calling to reach that beautiful destination.

Ask for help all the way, 'Lord, help me, I can't do this on my own', and it will be given. The human being has the capacity to love for a lifetime. Real, unconditional love, which is God-given. When this gift starts flowing in your life you will be victorious in Christ.

Be blessed!

Recommended Reading

Romans Chapter 12	Overcoming Evil

ACTIVITY 15

What is the term used for a Christian who walks away from their faith and goes back into the world? ....

How often will the Lord forgive you when you sin? ....

....

What is the unforgiveable sin? ....

....

Have you walked away from the Lord and, if yes, for how long? .....

....

....

What will you do or did you do to start finding your way back? .....

....

....

Describe God's love: ....

....

....

Notes: ....

....

....

....

....

....

....

This Journey

This journey that I have started
Is not for the faint-hearted
I stepped forward with great expectation
But will I ever reach my destination?
For You promised not that it would be easy
So I stay focussed and keep releasing
My faith in You, every chance I get
To help me never to forget
What You did for me at Calvary
To save my soul and set me free.

With great faith I could move mountains
But the trials of life flow like fountains
Bringing distractions in their wake
Never relenting, trying to make me break
Yet a still soft voice deep inside
Reminds me of who I am in Christ
A child of the light no more in darkness
Covered and protected in God's fortress
Once I began to call out to Him
He made me His dwelling place and entered in.

Weakness, no more a power over me
Fear, detached, unstrapped, now I'm free
With clarity I now perceive
The spiritual journey the world cannot conceive
Taking each moment in my stride
Overcoming each hurdle, I continue to strive
For perfection in my belief
That in God there is no grief
For every pain I experience
Become but a memory when I'm in His presence.

And this is where I will remain
Being saturated by His heavenly rain

For the treasures of heaven, He has poured out
And now in me there is no doubt
That He is the living God Supreme
Lord and Master over all living beings
Giving so much, but for many it was in vain
As they reject His coming, His suffering and His pain
But me, I continue to believe
That eternal life in Christ, I will receive.

SOURCES

The Amplified Bible
Scripture quotations taken from the Amplified® Bible (AMP), Copyright © 2015 by The Lockman Foundation. Used with permission. www.lockman.org

The King James Bible
Scriptures taken from the King James Bible

The New King James Bible
Scripture taken from the New King James Version®. Copyright © 1982 by Thomas Nelson. Used by permission. All rights reserved.

Nelson's Illustrated Dictionary of the Bible, Herbert Lockyer, Sr., Editor, Thomas Nelson, c1986

How to Pray Effectively: Volume 1, Pastor Chris Oyakhilome, Copyright © 2012, Loveworld Publishing

Due to the changing nature of the Internet, web addresses in this book may have changed since publication.

AUTHOR PROFILE

P. L. Bennett counsels and mentors new Christians starting out on their journey of faith. She teaches the Bible in a practical and easy to understand way. She reaches out to anyone struggling with their Christian faith, including those who have fallen away and are trying to find their way back, those who are curious and those who are seeking a simple, uncomplicated understanding of Christianity.

Drawing on her own life experiences, she teaches the new convert how to apply their faith to real life challenges and how to deal with the difficulties we all face. She teaches that Jesus is not just for the Christians, He is for the world and that everyone who seeks Him will find Him.

Patricia's inspiration to write is a lifelong passion that was realised in her first book *The Best Journey Ever: A Simple Guide Through Christianity*. She draws from the Christians she mentors who are unsure about their faith, why they were called and their daily struggles in finding purpose. Patricia continues to be guided by God in fulfilling her purpose and sharing her testimony.

Patricia has a bachelor's degree in Information Systems and Social Sciences from the University of the West of England and is an IT professional. She has one grown daughter and lives in the United Kingdom.

Her online platform:

Web: www.plbennett.org
Facebook: @plbennettministries
Instagram: @plbennett_official
Blog: www.watersinthewilderness.org
Linkedin: plbennettministries
Twitter: plbministries

What Did You Think of *The Best Journey Ever: A Simple Guide Through Christianity*?

A big thank you for purchasing this book. It means a lot that you chose this book specifically from such a wide range on offer. I do hope you enjoyed it.

Book reviews are incredibly important for an author. All feedback helps them improve their writing for future projects and for developing this edition. If you are able to spare a few minutes to post a review on Amazon then, from the bottom of my heart, thank you very much.

PUBLISHER INFORMATION

Rowanvale Books provides publishing services to independent authors, writers and poets all over the globe. We deliver a personal, honest and efficient service that allows authors to see their work published, while remaining in control of the process and retaining their creativity. By making publishing services available to authors in a cost-effective and ethical way, we at Rowanvale Books hope to ensure that the local, national and international community benefits from a steady stream of good quality literature.

For more information about us, our authors or our publications, please get in touch.

www.rowanvalebooks.com
info@rowanvalebooks.com

Lightning Source UK Ltd.
Milton Keynes UK
UKHW020630130421
381918UK00013B/951